Lincoln Public Library
May 1986

796.345

inside
badminton

inside badminton

irving l. finston
and
charles remsberg

Contemporary Books, Inc.
Chicago

Library of Congress Cataloging in Publication Data

Finston, Irving L.
　　Inside badminton.

　　Includes index.
　　1. Badminton (Game)　2. Badminton (Game)—
Rules.　I. Remsberg, Charles, joint author.
II. Title.
GV1007.F47　　1978　　796.34′5　　78-57467
ISBN 0-8092-7653-4
ISBN 0-8092-7652-6 pbk.

All photographs unless otherwise credited by Irving L. Finston.

Copyright © 1978 by Irving L. Finston and Charles Remsberg
All rights reserved
Published by Contemporary Books, Inc.
180 North Michigan Avenue, Chicago, Illinois 60601
Manufactured in the United States of America
Library of Congress Catalog Card Number:78-57467
International Standard Book Number: 0-8092-7653-4 (cloth)
　　　　　　　　　　　　　　　　　　0-8092-7652-6 (paper)

Published simultaneously in Canada by
Beaverbooks
953 Dillingham Road
Pickering, Ontario L1W 1Z7
Canada

contents

Introduction vii

1 Before You Play 1

2 Serving 13

3 Hitting Back 25

4 Playing to Win 47

5 Drill and Fitness 65

6 Club and Tournament Basics 71

7 USBA Rules 79

Glossary 87

Appendix 91

Index 97

introduction

Most people regard badminton as a gentle, noncompetitive, backyard diversion for sleepy summer afternoons. Yet those who have faced the game in its *best* setting—indoors on a breezeless court where the shuttlecock zips back and forth at astounding speeds and under great control—have discovered that badminton is something else, entirely.

It's fast, it's tricky, it's physically and mentally demanding. And in increasing numbers, it is attracting players of consummate skill, most of whom find the game more exciting and challenging than tennis. Without doubt, badminton is one of the most invigorating—and sometimes most infuriating—games in the sports world. Little wonder that in many countries, it is the first or second most popular sport played.

Badminton's roots reach back at least two-thousand years to the ancient Orient. It is vaguely related to an old children's game called "battledore and shuttlecock," which involved hitting weirdly shaped objects with small, crude racquets. The present-day version is believed to have started among British army personnel stationed in India. According to legend, a group of soldiers got drunk after dinner one evening, stuck feathers in a cork, and began batting the "bird" around. They called the game that quickly evolved "poona."

In the 1870s, British officers on home leave introduced poona at a house party at the country estate of the Duke of Beaufort in Gloucestershire. From then on, as the game rapidly spread throughout England, it was known by the name of the duke's estate, Badminton.

The halls or salons in which badminton was played in those days sometimes were scarcely larger than the court itself and were entered through center doors that opened inward. Consequently, the early courts were shaped like hour glasses, narrow in the middle at the net (and doors) and four feet broader at the base lines. The present rectangular shape, shorter and narrower than a tennis court, did not become official until the turn of the century.

Two players, Bayard Clark and E. Langdon Wilkes, brought badminton to the United States and formed the Badminton Club of the City of New York in the winter of 1878–1879. Membership was limited to single "gentlemen" and "good looking" single girls. Apparently, there was no abundance of either, for only 40 persons joined. Nonetheless, the club has endured as the oldest badminton organization in the world with continuous existence.

Today, indoor badminton is experiencing a welcome revival in the U.S., having lost out in popularity to the outdoor version in the 1930s. Fitness-conscious men and women are recognizing its remarkable capacity for trimming pounds and toning muscles. Those with a competitive streak appreciate the limitless opportunities for developing and polishing skills, and others just looking for a good time are finding that badminton is one of the most sociable sports around.

More than one hundred thousand Americans of all ages are currently involved in indoor badminton, and the number is growing daily. As tennis interest has begun to plateau, operators of public and private courts are converting more and more of their facilities to badminton use. Tournaments in high schools, colleges, and among the general population are proliferating, and some championship matches are now being televised. Some observers predict that badminton is on its way to becoming the next recreational craze.

Whether you're a new player or one who has been at the game for years, this book can help you. It covers every funda-

Men's doubles action—defending team is standing side by side. *Courtesy Travelers Insurance Companies*

mental you need to know to build yourself into an excellent player. You can learn—or refresh your understanding of—how to serve to put yourself at best advantage, what strokes to use when the volleys get fast and furious, what drills and exercises can make you a more formidable player, all the rules necessary for proper play, guidelines for organizing a tournament—and much more.

Irv Finston is a director and former officer of the Midwest Badminton Association; Chuck Remsberg an active member and former officer of the Badminton Club of Evanston, Illinois. The advice we offer in *Inside Badminton* is based not only on our own experience in more than a decade of playing, coaching, and running tournaments, but also on the knowledge and experience of badminton champions we have seen in action and, in some cases, have had the privilege of playing against. These include Rahul Naidu, 1977 United States Badminton Association men's junior national doubles champion; Bruce Pontow, 1977 and 1978 national mixed doubles champ; Mike Adams, 1975 national men's singles champion; and Pam Bristol, 1977 national women's singles champion and 1977 and 1978 national mixed doubles champion.

sistance to: Cletus Eli and Virginia Lyon, USBA president and former president respectively; Jim Wigglesworth and Harold Deeman, president and former president respectively of the Midwest Badminton Association; and Jack Van Praag, an international figure in the sport.

As you absorb the pages ahead, you'll become aware of the fact that badminton is deceptive—not just in reputation, but in the play itself. Deception is this game's core ingredient. Any and every stroke can produce fresh surprises—and the more you know about the basics, the better equipped you'll be to deliver and cope with the tactics of winning.

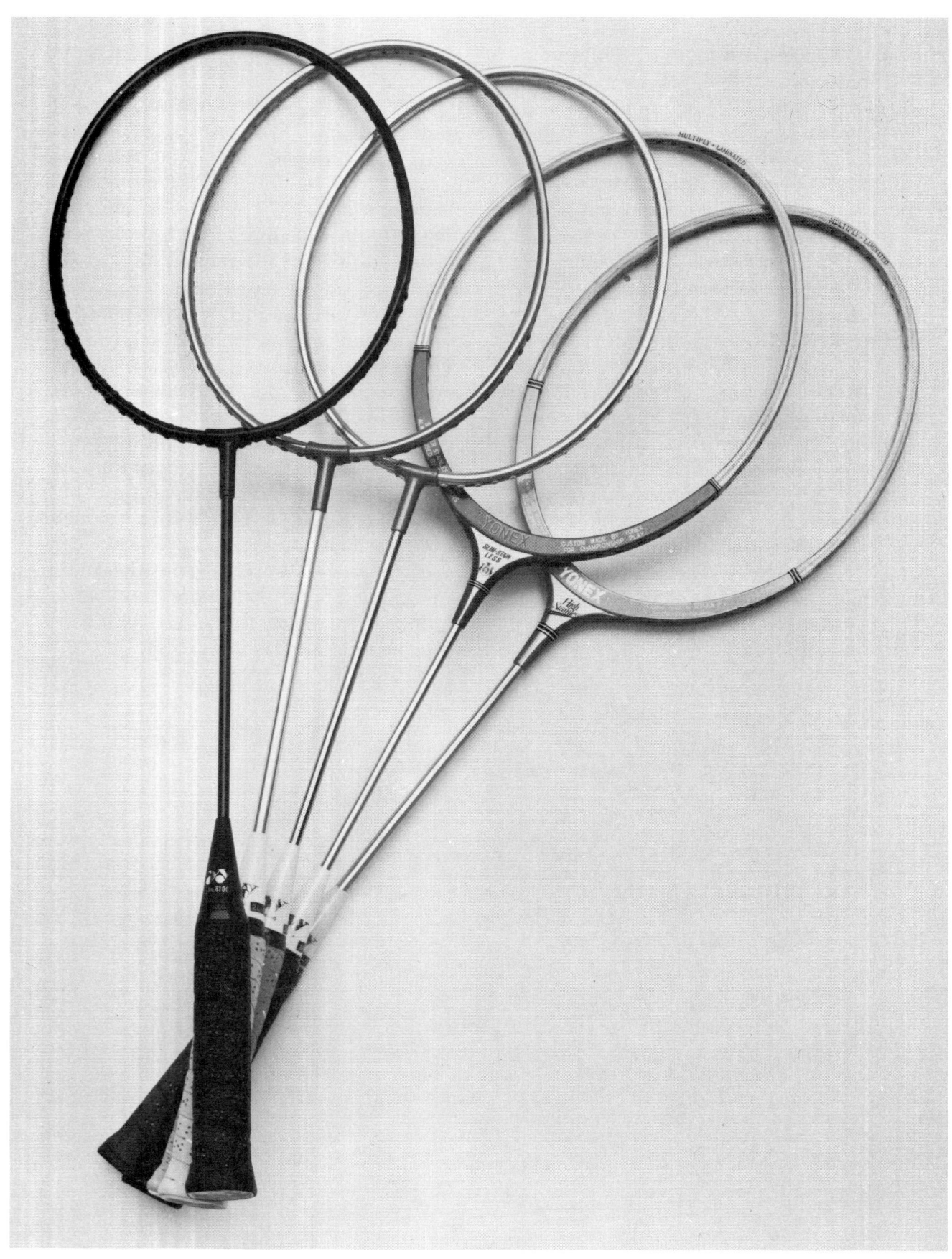

UNSTRUNG WOOD AND METAL FRAMES.
Courtesy Yonex Company

chapter 1
BEFORE YOU PLAY

Whatever your age or skill, there's a place for you in badminton. Hospitality is part of the code among experienced players. Most will be eager to help you polish your game, even if you're a beginner.

This is one of the few sports left in which even the champions earn their livings at something else and come to the game seeking rewards other than money and fame. A haven from fast-buck commercialism, badminton has always relied heavily upon and been deeply involved with amateurs. And that makes playing it much more enjoyable.

Badminton's basic concept is simple. In singles, you play alone against an opponent; in doubles, you and a partner stand another team of two. A shuttlecock or bird is served into the air with a racquet and is hit back and forth over a net that spans the middle of the court. The object is to place your shots so your opponent misses the bird entirely, hits it into or short of the net, or hits it out of bounds.

Frequently this happens by sheer luck. But consistent winning requires planning, anticipation, control, and a knack for deception. These can be developed only with a great deal of practice and, most important, in the hot crucible of play.

We'll show you step by step what you need to know to master all these essentials. The practice, of course, is up to you.

THE COURT

The badminton court is a rectangle, with the boundaries for a game dependent upon whether singles or doubles are being played. Usually the boundaries for both games are marked on the same surface with lines that are 1½ inches wide. Those lines not applicable are simply ignored during any given game.

For singles, the court is 44 feet long and 17 feet wide. The length is the same for doubles, but the width is expanded to 20 feet. For both, a net is stretched across the exact middle of the court. Its tape, or

2 BEFORE YOU PLAY

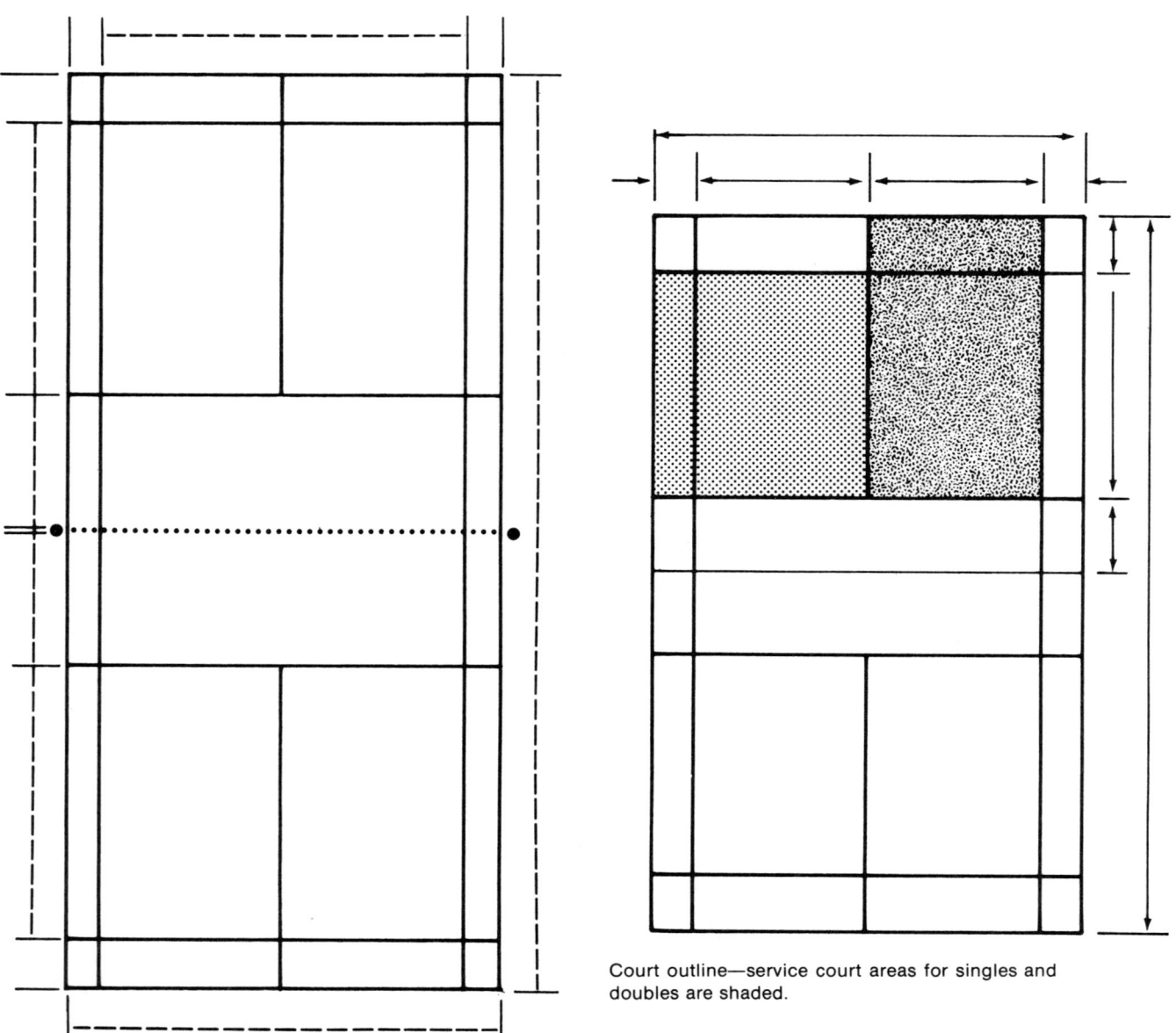

Court outline for singles and doubles.

Court outline—service court areas for singles and doubles are shaded.

top edge, should be 5 feet above the playing surface. To prevent claustrophobia and to give players plenty of swinging and running room, an apron of about 5 feet should be cleared on all sides of the court.

Some markings on the court pertain only when serving the bird or receiving a serve. These are the short service line, applicable in both singles and doubles, and the long service line (also called inner base line), applicable only in doubles. How these lines figure in the game will be explained in Chapter 2.

Because the slightest wind affects the flight of the bird and thus hampers precision and finesse, indoor courts are far preferable to outdoor. Also they permit year-around play, regardless of climate. All official badminton competitions are held inside, and the principles of this book can most readily be used by indoor players. However, if you just want a little fun and exercise and the weather is nice, you'll find badminton a very portable game. You can improvise a court quickly on the beach, on your driveway, or on a level lawn. With extra practice, you can even develop an impressive style out of doors. In Malaya, an area that has produced many international champions, badminton is played almost exclusively in the open air.

If you can play inside, though, try it. You'll discover it's a whole different game.

If the ceiling is about 26 feet high—enough to accommodate the lofty, arcing shots that are so common and crucial in badminton—a court can be laid out in virtually any enclosure: a gym, a church hall, a fieldhouse, a barn. Lacking metal posts or wall hooks, you can even hang a net from two-by-twos stuck in cans of concrete. Fine equipment may improve your game, but this is one sport in which it is not required.

Court lighting should come from a source that does not glare or reflect into players' eyes. Because the game is vigorous and heat affects the speed and flight patterns of some birds, room temperatures in the 50s or 60s are considered ideal. A smooth wooden floor, clear of obstacles and hazards, makes the most comfortable court surface.

THE RACQUET

There's nothing badminton buffs prize more than their racquets, and they'll be quick to defend the choice made from among the various possibilities. You'll hear impassioned testimonials to both metal and wood racquets and vigorous assertions about how an expensive new racquet changed somebody's game. Some players show up courtside with an array of personal racquets that would shame a salesman's sample case.

Keep in mind that a racquet is only a tool. You must provide the talent to use it correctly. A player who really knows his or her game can capitalize on the strengths and overcome the weaknesses of practically any racquet.

It is wise, though, to avoid racquets that retail for less than $15. Cheaper models tend to warp if strung tightly and are easily cracked or broken. We've seen some drugstore models fall apart in the playing of a single game!

Your best bet is to try out several and choose the one you're most comfortable handling. Championships have been won with wooden racquets, metal racquets, and combinations of the two.

Oddly, there are no rules specifying the size, weight, and shape of a badminton racquet. You could use a two-by-four to swing at the bird, although you'd probably be at a severe disadvantage.

The "accepted" racquet is 26 inches long and vaguely resembles a tennis racquet. However, its slightly oval head is

4 BEFORE YOU PLAY

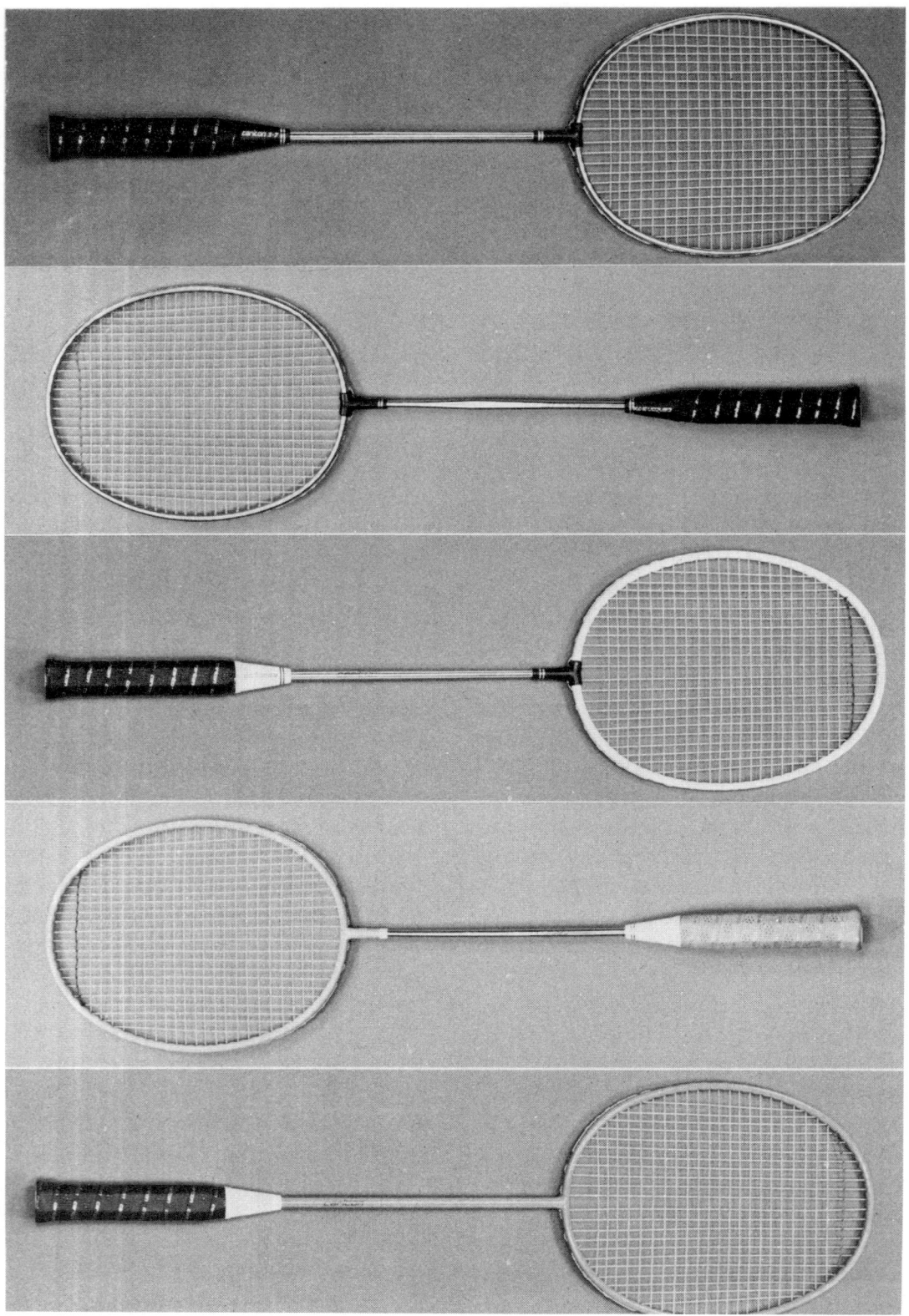

METAL RACQUETS. *Courtesy Carlton Company*

smaller, its cylindrical shaft is thinner, and the racquet itself is much lighter and less awkward. This lightness is important because it makes possible easy wrist flexibility which, as you'll see, is a great part of this game.

Metal racquets usually weigh between 3.7 and 4.3 ounces, wooden ones about 4.7 to 5.5 ounces. A heavier racquet offers more hitting power, but is slower in stroking. On the other hand, some players feel that a light but rigid metal racquet lacks response, the "life," and delicate touch provided by wood. Consequently, some manufacturers have designed metal racquets—for example, the Carlton 3.7X—with a slightly flattened shaft. This adds a whip to your stroke, similar to what you can achieve with a good Vicort or Yonex wood racquet.

The racquet's thin, netted strings are generally gut or nylon and should be strung at a tension of about 15 to 18 pounds. Quality strings will add considerably to your ability to direct the bird. If you want to avoid the expense of gut, Ashaway nylon strings are a consistently safe buy.

In testing a racquet, pay particular attention to the grip. Make sure you can hold it comfortably, without clutching tightly. The grip should not be so big around that you can't easily encircle it with your hand or so small that your fingers overlap to the base of your thumb.

If you choose a wooden racquet, be sure to keep it in a press when not in use to prevent warping. Some people carry the racquet to the court in a press, but that defeats the purpose. The press should be kept at home in a place where temperature and humidity are relatively constant. Carry your racquet in a waterproof cover. If the racquet does get wet, dry it off carefully and return it to the press as soon as practical.

THE BIRD

There is considerably less controversy about badminton birds than about racquets. Nearly every experienced player prefers the traditional feathered bird. It weighs about 5 or 6 grams and consists of a cork button, or head, into which 14 to 16 trimmed, 2½-inch-long goose feathers are stuck like a crown.

Light as it is, this missile will fly slower than any object hit in any other sport, if tapped gently. Walloped, it can rocket off a racquet at speeds more than 110 mph. Yet because its feathers fan out in flight, the bird can decelerate rapidly and drop precipitiously. The vagaries of its behavior are a large part of the game's enjoyment—and heartache.

Feathered birds are expensive, however—upwards of $11 per dozen—and tend to tatter with play. In tournaments, it's not unusual for players to go through two or three feathered birds in a single game.

For economic reasons, less expensive birds with rubberized buttons and crowns of perforated plastic or nylon have become common in nontournament games. The United States Badminton Association has even approved specified Carlton synthetic birds for some junior and B-level tournaments. Synthetic birds come in a variety of weights and speeds, the heavier and faster ones suitable for outdoor play. Good ones cost about $7 a dozen and can last through many games. Still, experienced players insist that synthetics lack the appealing characteristics of feathered birds, branding them variously as "too dead," "too fast," and "too uncontrollable."

If you can afford feathers, fine. Aeroplane, Sportcraft, the H. I., Pioneer, and Yonex are some of the top brands. We agree they contribute to a more exotic

6   BEFORE YOU PLAY

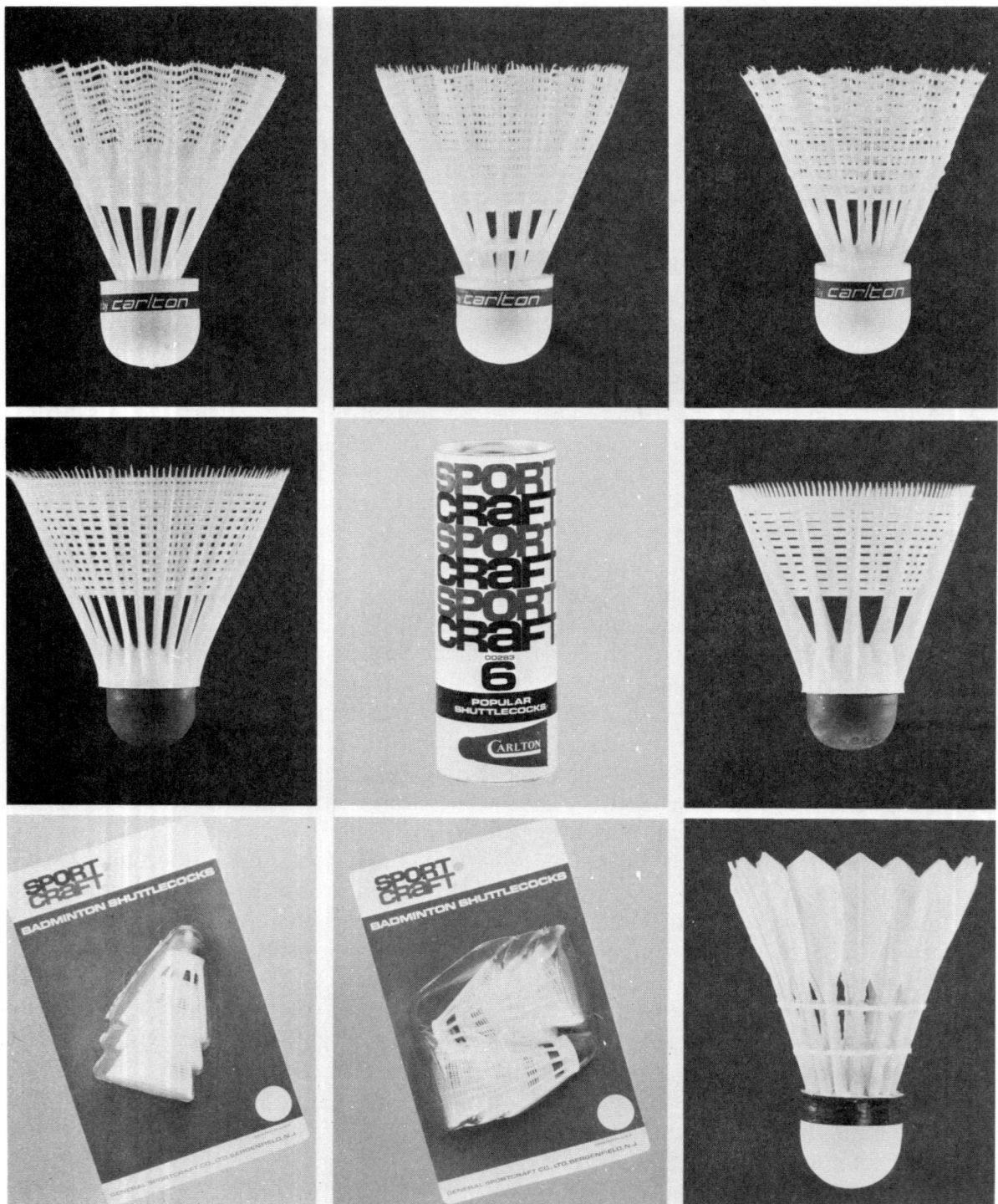

PLASTIC AND FEATHER BIRDS. *Courtesy Carlton and Sportcraft companies*

game. A skilled player can make a feathered bird virtually climb over the top of the net to score a point—a feat of rare beauty. But if you can't pay the freight, don't fret. A good synthetic bird—like Carlton's "tournament grade"—offers plenty of challenge for the average player.

Besides costing more, feathered birds take more pampering. A synthetic bird is merely shaken out of the tube you bought it in and you're ready to play. But a feathered bird must be carefully humidified before a game to draw enough water into its feathers so they won't be brittle and break easily, but not so much that they become waterlogged.

Players frequently have their own jealously guarded humidification formulas. In one method the birds are removed from their storage tube a day before play and stood on their feathered edges in a tub in about a quarter-inch of water. After 15 minutes, they are placed back into the tube and it is in turn wrapped in a sealed plastic trash bag. The birds are removed just before play. A less complicated method is to wrap a wet cloth around the unopened tube and put the tube in a sealed plastic bag a day before play. Either way works fine.

Whether you use a feathered or synthetic bird, you should always test it before playing. Stand in back of the base line and slam the bird using full strength toward the opposite court with a high, underhand shot. If it lands 12 to 18 inches in front of the opposing base line, you have a fine, playable bird. If it goes beyond, it's a "fast" bird and can be slowed slightly by carefully bending out the tips of the feathers. If it falls short of the target area, either it's too slow or dead and should be abandoned—or you need work to strengthen your stroke.

PROPER CLOTHING

A maxim of badminton is "White is right." White-only is not mandatory, but it is preferred and it's requested in most tournament play. Whatever colors you choose, dress conservatively. Modest, tasteful clothing is one of the game's lingering touches of gentility.

Comfort and safety are important considerations in choosing your garb. Because of the swinging, running, and stretching, you'll want something loose-fitting, but not so baggy that it interferes with your game or threatens to trip you. In nontournament play, some people wear sweatsuits or warm-up jackets; others favor tennis outfits, slacks, or bermuda shorts. It's considered bad taste to go shirtless.

Shoes should be carefully selected. Tennis shoes with rubber soles are best, but the soles should allow some sliding to avoid ankle turning. Abrupt starting, stopping, and pivoting put heavy stress on your feet, so your shoes should fit well and provide good arch support and substantial sole cushioning. You may want to wear two pair of heavy wool socks for extra padding.

Never play barefoot, even on grass. This increases the danger of slipping and of turning a foot under and tearing a tendon.

Many players wear sweatbands on forehead or wrist. They're well worth their slight price, for nothing is more disconcerting than a trickle of sweat running into your eyes or slicking your grip on the racquet as you're about to make a shot. Don't get the bands too tight, though, or they'll annoy you and, in the case of the headband, may cause a headache.

THE GAME

The rotation of play and the scoring in badminton are unlike any other racquet sport. They're a realm unto themselves, with intricacies and idiosyncrasies befitting badminton's English heritage.

Some people unschooled in the basics think badminton is a version of tennis. Both games involve the use of racquets to bat a missile over a net, both have a court with specified boundaries, and both can be played by two or four people. But there the similarities largely end.

Unlike tennis, the rules of badminton require that the flying object be hit before it falls to ground. Once the bird touches the court floor, the rally is over. Moreover, you can score points only when you are serving. Rallies often are fought long and hard with no points whatever being scored when the exhausting action ends.

Beyond these simple facts, things get more complicated. For instance, rotation of play depends on the type of game you're playing, and the score required to win can differ with what sex you are. But hang in! Once you understand them, you won't forget the complexities and you'll find in playing that the game actually progresses quite naturally.

Singles Rotation

In a singles game, a server hits the bird from his service court into the receiving box of his opponent. Serves always are cross-court, or diagonal. If the bird would fall in-bounds were it allowed to drop to the floor, the receiver must hit it back over the net or the server automatically scores a point. Once the bird is returned, the volley continues back and forth until one player commits a fault; that is, fails to get the bird over the net or hits it out of bounds.

If you're serving and your opponent commits the fault, you win one point and continue serving until you yourself fault. When you fault, you forfeit the serve to your opponent, who then gets a crack at winning points. When he or she faults, it's your turn again. And so on.

Each player's initial serve in the game is made from the right-hand court. But after that, service alternates between right- and left-hand serving areas.

When it's your turn to serve any time after your first one of the game, you must start your service from the side of the court from where you served last. In other words, if your score is 0 or an even number, resume serving from the right-hand serving court. If your score is an odd number, start from your left-hand court.

Doubles Rotation

A doubles player continues serving so long as he or she is winning points, just as in singles. However, a fault by the doubles server *or* partner means loss of the serve.

At the very beginning of a doubles game, the side that serves first is allowed only one fault before it must relinquish service. After that, *each* player on a side gets a chance to serve and fault before service passes to the opposing team.

Whenever service transfers to a new team, that side's first serve is *always* delivered from the right-hand court. The server then alternates between right- and left-hand service courts so long as he or she continues to score. As the server moves from one to the other, the partner moves, too, to defend unprotected areas of the court. The receiving side, however, does not shift its positions with each serve.

When a side's first server loses the serve, that person is said to be *down*. If service came last from the left-hand court, the partner then begins service on the right, and vice versa. When both partners are down, their inning is over, and they surrender service for the moment. They retain the court positions occupied on the last serve as they now become receivers.

Between the switching on each serve

Backhand drop with defenders side by side. *Courtesy Travelers Insurance Companies*

and all the running around that usually occurs during a rally, doubles players sometimes have trouble remembering their position for making or receiving a serve. Your score will help you figure that out. If at the start of the game you were in the right-hand court—that is, if you were making or receiving the first serve— you should always be in the right-hand court whenever a serve is being made and your side's score is 0 or an even number. You're what's called the even player. If you start the game on the left, you're the odd player. You should be in the right-hand court to make or take a serve *only* when your side's score is an odd number.

Scoring

In men's singles and all doubles, the first side to win 15 points wins the game. In women's singles, the game is 11 points. This is a chauvinistic legacy of badminton's nineteenth century background, when the "fair sex" was thought too frail to match men's endurance. In practice today, the 11-point limit on women's singles usually means that these contests are the most savagely fought of all, because there is less time to recover from your own mistakes and your opponent's strong assaults.

Actually, if players in any kind of game want a shorter or longer contest, they can set a different winning score before play begins. Games of 21 points are common in doubles and even, in fact, in women's singles.

Ties near the end of a game can cause revisions in the number of points necessary for victory. In a 15-point game, if the score becomes tied at 13, the side that first won 13 points has the option of setting the game at 5 additional points. If they take the option, the score immediately becomes 0-0 (or "love-all") and the first side to reach 5 wins. In a tie at 14, a game can be set at 3 additional points. (In a 21-point game, 3- and 5-point sets can be made when the score is tied at 19 and 20 respectively.) In women's singles, the game can be set at 3 additional points if a tie occurs at 9, 2 additional points at 10-all.

Badminton games can stand by themselves, or three games can be grouped together into a match, or rubber. In a match, the side that scores the best in two out of the three games wins. Match players change courts at the end of each of the first two games. In the third, they switch at 8 points for men and 6 for women in standard games, or at 11 in a 21-point game. The side that won the previous game serves first for each new one.

Good sportsmanship is an integral part of the game: everyone shakes hands at the conclusion of a match.

ETIQUETTE

Badminton's country estate origins have imposed something else besides its complicated codified rules: an unspoken agreement that while players compete like sharks and try mercilessly to destroy each other on court, they do so with good manners, cordiality, and civility.

Court etiquette demands introductions all around before you start to play, if there are strangers in your group. During the game, you should compliment aloud unusually good shots made by your partner or opponent and now and then call out "*Good eye!*" if someone accurately preceived that a hard-to-read bird was going to fall out of bounds. Under no circumstances should you yell at your opponent or otherwise try deliberately to distract him or her during play. At the end, everyone should shake hands and thank each other for a game well-played, even if it wasn't. Gloating, angrily throwing your racquet, or snobbishly refusing to play with persons less skilled than yourself are especially frowned upon.

In tournaments, linesmen are stationed at the court's perimeters to call birds in or out of bounds. Other times, players must assume this responsibility themselves. The player nearest where the bird lands should call it "good" or "bad." If you're the one, call objectively, even if it's to your disadvantage. Your word should be accepted without question. If no one is certain whether the bird landed in or out, it should be replayed. In making calls, remember that a bird is considered in-bounds if its button hits the line when it falls.

The honor system is also in effect where throwing a bird is concerned. That means carrying it forward or slinging it with your racquet instead of hitting it cleanly. This maneuver is a fault and, when admitted, ends the rally.

If in hitting a bird you inadvertently send it sailing onto a nearby court, wait until the rally on that court is over before stepping in to retrieve it. Wait off the apron so you create the least possible distraction for those players.

In tournaments, there is an umpire to tally and report scores. In normal play, though, players keep track themselves. It's proper for the server to call out the score before each serve, giving his or her own side's score first. In doubles, the number of downs a side has should also be indicated, after the score. A call of "10-6-1," for example, means the serving side has 10, the opposition 6, and the first server has already faulted.

When a bird that could decide the game is about to be served—in other words, the one that could make the fifteenth point in a 15-point game—it is courteous for the server to draw everyone's attention to the importance of the moment by calling out "Game bird" or "Game point."

Perhaps the least favorite badminton player is the "court hog." Often courts are in short supply and people are waiting beyond the apron to play. Under such circumstances, you should never keep control of a court for longer than one match without offering to relinquish it.

There's really nothing arcane about badminton's etiquette. The right conduct is just common courtesy. But close adherence to it can save you hassles and arguments—and leave you free to concentrate fully on playing the best game possible.

Ladies' singles service originating close to the net. *Courtesy Travelers Insurance Companies*

chapter 2
SERVING

The strokes used in service are unlike any other strokes in badminton, and the badminton serve is unlike any other service in the sports world. The restrictions making the serve legal are rather complex, involving even how you hold the racquet. You get no "second serve," as you do in tennis, so if you muff that first stroke it can mean the end of your chance to score points in that inning. Even if you do serve correctly, the stroke usually leaves you immediately on the defensive. In short, when you take position to put that bird into play, you're in probably the toughest—and most important—spot in the badminton game.

What you strive for first and foremost under these difficult circumstances is a delivery that will keep you from getting killed with a good return. You must think through your delivery before starting it, or an alert opponent will gleefully take advantage of you. If you plan well, however, you may be able to catch your opponent off-guard and score a quick point at his expense without the risks of a rally.

RULES OF SERVING

You can decide who serves first in a game by flipping a coin, but the true cognoscenti like to twirl a racquet on its head and let it fall to the floor. The player (or team) not doing the spinnng calls out "Rough" or "Smooth" during the twirl. When the racquet lands, either its "smooth" or "rough" side—that is, the smooth strands of the knots used to tie off the strings or their rough-cut ends—will be facing up. If the fall has been called correctly, that player (or team) has the right to initiate service. Since only servers can score, it's usually a good option to take.

The first serve in any game is always made from the right-hand service court to the receiving box or receiving court diagonally opposite. Subsequent rotation of service depends on whether a point is won or lost on the serve and whether you are playing singles or doubles, as explained in Chapter 1.

The boundaries of the serving and receiving areas also depend on the type of game. To serve in singles, you must stand within the rectangle formed by the short service line, the singles side line, the base line, and the center line. The boundaries of your opponent's receiving, or fair-fall, area are the same, but cross-court. In doubles, the serving and receiving areas are more nearly square. Each is encompassed by the short service line, the doubles side line, the short service (or inner base) line, and the center line in the appropriate court. An easy way to remember this is to think of the serving and receiving areas in singles as being long and narrow; in doubles, short and wide.

For your serve to be legal, you must strike the bird while it is below your waist. In addition, the entire racquet head must be discernibly below the whole of your racquet hand at the moment of impact. This is to keep you from taking an easy advantage as server. If the serve were made from a different position, say chest height or above, one could easily send the bird whizzing at the receiver at such high velocity and at such an angle that the receiver would be virtually compelled to hit it up, immediately providing an opportunity to smash down for a quick point. The hand rules keep things more nearly in balance.

There are foot rules, too. Should you step on or over your boundary lines while serving, the serve is illegal and you must surrender service to the next player without scoring that point. If your opponent steps on or out of the boundaries while awaiting the serve, he commits a fault and it's your point automatically. Once the bird leaves your racquet, however, all players can move anywhere they choose, irrespective of boundaries.

If your opponent allows your served bird to fall to the floor of his court unhit and it lands outside his receiving boundaries, you lose the point and service. If it lands in-bounds, you gain the point and move to your next serving position. The receiving area's boundary lines themselves are considered to be in-bounds, so if the button of the bird strikes a line when it lands, it's a fair serve.

A serve into the net is your loss; you don't get another chance. If, however, the bird hits the net but still flies into the proper receiving area, the serve is fair and should be played. This is not considered a let, as in tennis. If you try to serve but miss the bird entirely—don't even brush its feathers—you can try again.

In the event someone interferes with your serve or some foreign object (such as a bird from a nearby game) flies onto the court and distracts you or your opponent, a let may be called. The serve should be repeated as a standard courtesy, so long as the privilege is not abused.

Only the person who is the intended receiver may return the serve under any circumstances. If in doubles, for example, the player you serve to misses the bird and his or her partner swings and returns the serve, that's a fault—and your point. After the serve is returned, of course, any player on a side can take any shot.

SINGLES SERVE

Occasionally in singles you'll want to deliver a short serve to the fore part of your opponent's receiving box, just to "make a good citizen of him," as they say in badminton. It's a good idea in both singles and doubles to mix your serves a bit, so you don't become so predictable that your opponent is always prepared for what's next. Remember, the innermost

SERVING

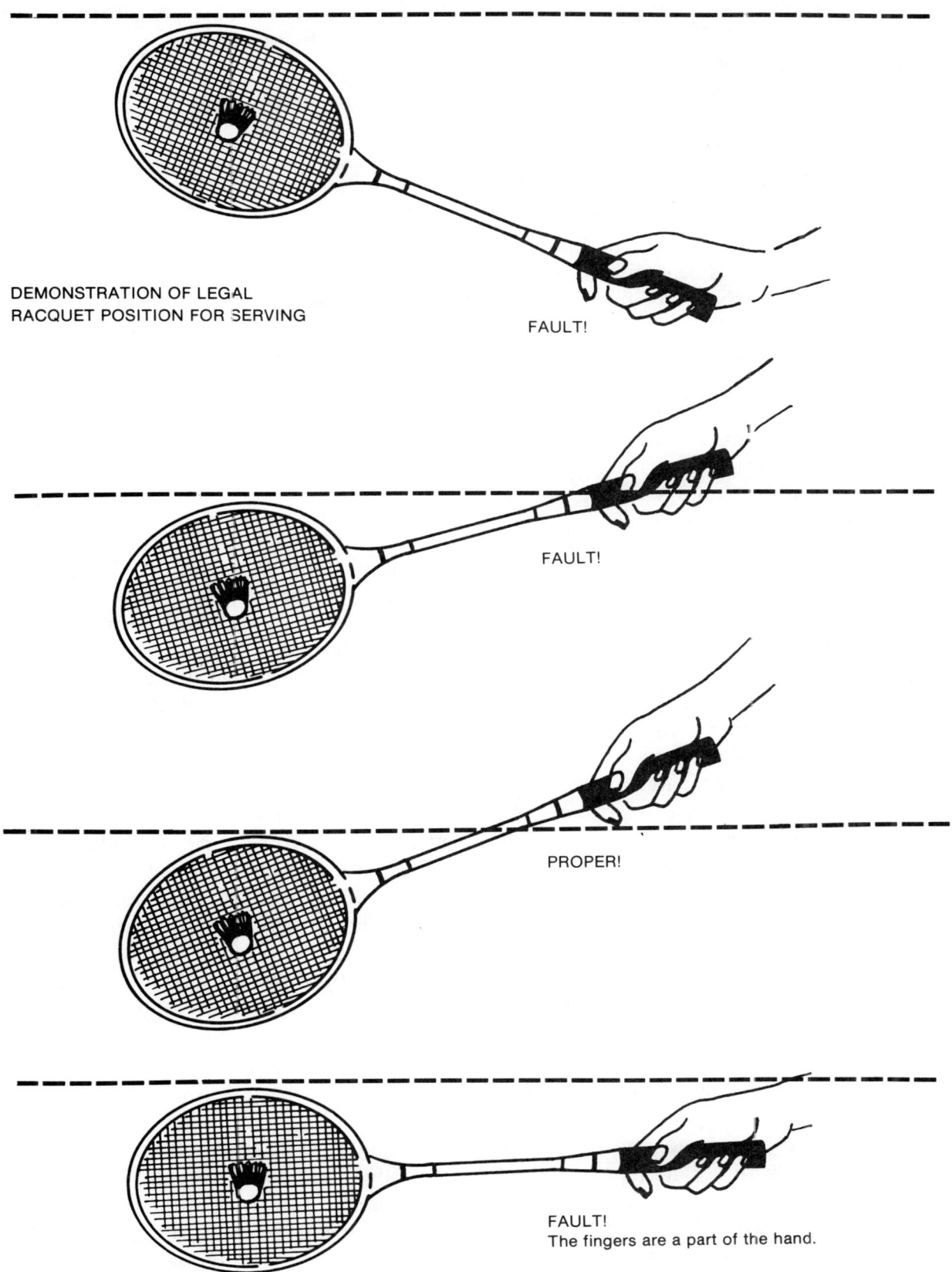

secret of this game is always deception, and variety is an important form of it.

Ordinarily, though, the singles serve is a high, arcing shot, designed to fall sharply at your opponent's base line. You will—or should—use this serve more often than not because it has two strong advantages for you as a server:

1) The receiver cannot return this serve with a smash, a devastating shot hit sharply and powerfully downward to the floor of your court. The dimensions of the court and the laws of physics conspire to make an attempted smash from the base line a sure loser, because the bird will go into the net. 2) The returns your opponent can use successfully on this serve are slower shots, which give you time to get ready for them. This time can be counted in seconds or fractions of seconds, but it can make all the difference in the rally to come.

The returns your opponent can use and that you, too, can subsequently employ in response will be discussed in Chapter 3. Here we're concerned only with the techniques of successful service.

Delivering the high singles serve with enough power and aim to reach your opponent's base line requires considerable practice, but success is essential. If you hit a high serve that reaches only to midcourt or forecourt, he or she *can* smash. Moreover, your opponent will have quickly determined your vulnerability and be ready every time.

Grip

For the singles serve, hold your racquet in the basic forehand grip. The racquet should lie in your hand as if you are shaking hands with it. The handle should be diagonally across your fingers, rather than in your palm. Don't bunch your fingers or clutch the racquet like a club.

You need a certain ease and flexibility for maximum effectiveness.

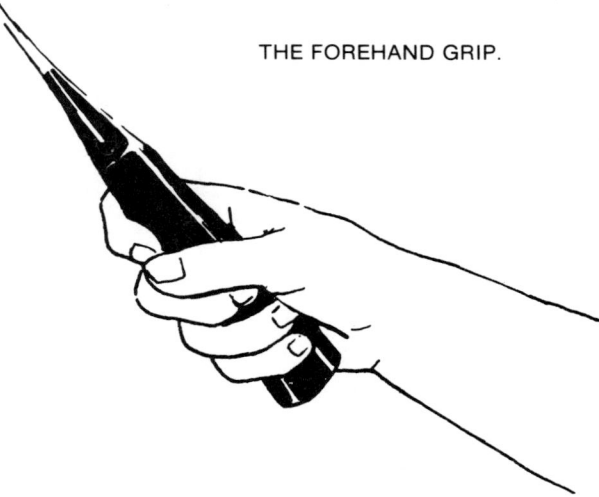
THE FOREHAND GRIP.

Stance

Stand in your service court close to the center line, about five-eighths or three-quarters of the way back from the net toward your base line. (If, in practicing, you've discovered you just don't have the power to deliver a serve fully to the opposition's base line from this position, stand closer to the net. If you have excess power, stand farther back.)

Keep your feet about shoulder width apart and, if you are right-handed, point your left shoulder toward your opponent's receiving court. Your weight should be on the balls of the feet, with your left foot forward.

Grasp the bird by its button between your left thumb and forefinger, with the feathers up. Keep this arm in front of your body, your elbow bent.

Swing

The singles serve should be delivered with a motion that involves your whole body to impel the bird with maximum force.

Rock from the balls of your feet back to your heels, shifting your balance and

SERVING 17

Even though fashion objects most players hold the bird as they wish.

weight. At the same time, bring your racquet arm back in an underhand swing so that your racquet and arm are almost parallel to the floor behind you.

Without interrupting your motion, let the bird fall and swing your racquet forward so you strike the bird as it is just above your left ankle. As you hit, bring your right foot forward and throw the kinetic energy of your whole body into the serve. The strong muscles of your thigh and calf will provide much of the power behind the bird, easing the strain on your arms and shoulders. The forehand grip allows a slight twist to the stroke, adding more strength.

Follow-through

Step forward with your right foot and let your racquet arm complete its upward arc, ending just in front of your face with the racquet above your left shoulder. Now you need only lower your racquet slightly and you are ready for your opponent's return.

If you served from the midcourt position, you're ideally situated to run forward, backward, or to either side to intercept whatever shot he returns. If you were nearer or farther from the net, be prepared to pivot and run backwards or dash forward as your opponent's shot demands.

DOUBLES SERVES

One of the big problems most beginners have in doubles is avoiding collisions with their partners as action develops during the rally. It's a good idea before the game to confer with your partner and decide whether your basic strategy for covering the court will be side by side, front and back, or rotation. These strategies will be discussed in detail in Chapter 4. Selecting one will help determine where your partner should stand when you are serving and where you will move immediately upon completing service.

You'll have more opportunity in doubles than in singles to inject variety and deception in your service. There's nothing like a mixed bag of serves for keeping your opponent in the proper state of anxiety. If you can catch him or her expecting a short serve when you deliver a long one, you may experience the inestimable pleasure of seeing your opponent rush to the net for the return and then, flat-footed, sadly watch the bird sail overhead, beyond reach.

Your repertoire of doubles serves should include the following.

The singles serve.

Various positions for men's and women's doubles (but not mixed doubles).

20 SERVING

Mixed doubles serve and position for partners.

The Standard

The standard doubles serve is delivered underhand with the same forehand grip, the same foot position, and the same swing as the high singles serve, but with altogether different power and intent. In doubles, this serve should be a mild, almost meek stroke, not the all-out energy explosion called for in singles. By delivering the serve gently, you can "kiss" the bird over the net rather than blast it.

Delivery is made from just behind the short service line, usually in the corner where it intersects with the center line. Instead of aiming for the base line, as in singles, the standard serve's intent is to have the bird merely skim the net. If allowed to fall, it should hit your opponent's short service line or just beyond it. You are trying to get the receiver to hit up, or "lift" the bird in making the return so that you'll be able to smash it down for a fast and emphatic conclusion to the rally.

It takes considerable practice to learn

to keep the bird very low in going over the net. This is essential, of course, to discourage a smash return. To compensate, until you get this serve mastered, you'll find it helpful to serve from a position closer to the side line to flatten out the arc of the bird's flight path. Be prepared, though, to move quickly back toward the center line for the return, if necessary.

Hold the bird by the tip for service.

As server, you should eventually learn to follow your serve toward the net after the bird is in play, so you can defend against short returns. You'll need some experience to tell what your optimum position is for handling net shots. Most players prefer about 3 feet back from the net, with their bodies flexible enough to pivot toward one side line or reach toward the other, depending on where the return comes.

Remember after you serve to keep your racquet up, with the handle about chest height, ready for the return.

The Flick

The flick serve is midway, both in targeting and delivery power, between the standard serve and the high singles serve. Court position and body movement are the same as for the standard, but you should try having the bird land near your opponent's long service line and to fly in as high an arc as possible to get there.

The flick is most useful when your opponent's body language is telegraphing the clear message that he or she is anticipating a standard serve and is itching to rush the net to intercept it. Delivered correctly, the bird will travel above the head as he or she starts toward the net and will drop fast enough to prevent reversing course and reaching it in time. Some outstanding players may be able to backpedal and return a flick with a stroke between their legs or from behind their backs just before the bird touches ground, but the average player won't stand a chance.

Beware, though: this serve is very vulnerable to a smash return. If you read your opponent wrong, he or she may simply stand ground and smash your flick down your side line, making you the one who can't reach it in time.

The Drive

The drive is a fast, mean serve. You deliver it long and low from the outer boundary of the court, well back from the short service line.

You employ essentially the same underhand delivery and body movement as in the other serves, but the bird should be hit slightly more sidearm. That is, both the racquet and the bird must be held out to your right side, if you are right-handed. Remember the rule, though, about keeping the racquet head below your hand and the bird below your waist at impact.

Try to keep the trajectory or flight angle low, but give your stroke much more power than in the other doubles serves—enough to carry the bird to the inner back corner of the receiving box.

Executed fast enough and low enough, this is a terrific shot. The bird tends to fly outside the receiving area until just the last moment, and the receiver is kept wondering whether to chance that it will ultimately fall outside the lines or to attempt a return.

You can enhance the innate viciousness of the shot by hitting it hard and directly at your opponent so he or she must make a hurried, awkward return stroke which may conveniently set up a nice return shot. Drive serves directed at your opponent's chest or face can be particularly intimidating.

The Backhand

Of all the doubles serves, the most sophisticated and probably most favored by top badminton talent is the backhand serve, introduced by players from the Orient. It's exceptionally useful and effective because it can present the bird on an almost flat trajectory. This, combined with its speed, severely limits the return possibilities.

To deliver this serve, stand in the corner where the short service and center lines intersect, squarely facing your opponent, with feet flat. Hold your racquet in the backhand grip, which is the same as the forehand except that the handle is turned slightly so that you can lay your thumb along its wide side. Raise your

Backhand serve with partner in proper position.

racquet handle up beneath your chin so the racquet head is pointing straight down and is well below your waist.

Hold the bird, feathers up, directly in front of the racquet face. Arch your body slightly, release the bird and, with a flick of your racquet wrist, shoot the bird into a drive serve to your opponent.

The big risk here is a fault by serving the bird into the net. You'll need practice to overcome that hazard, but once you

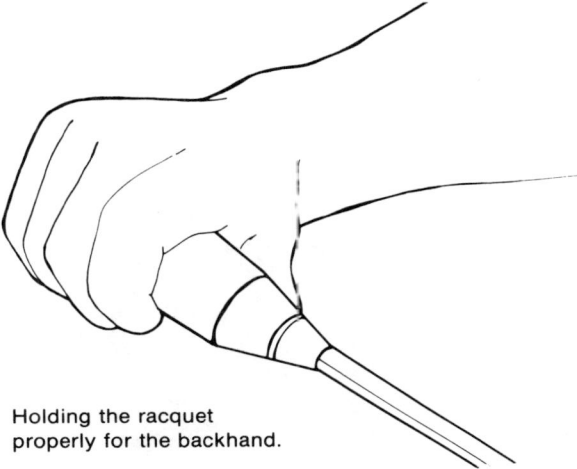

Holding the racquet properly for the backhand.

have you'll find that this serve can provide a marvelous edge in a tight match.

SERVING STRATEGY

The deception that inevitably becomes part of a good badminton game can begin the instant the bird is served. Most top players develop serves in which the bird's line of fall brushes perilously close to a boundary line. This is a strategy you'll find rewarding to cultivate.

If you can serve in such a way that your opponent *thinks* the bird is headed out of bounds, you may bluff him or her into not attempting a return. If it then falls to the floor inside the box, the point is yours. Similarly, you may lure your opponent into swinging at birds that otherwise would fall out of bounds and cause a loss of service. If the racquet so much as brushes the bird, it is considered a hit. If the hit is too weak to send the bird back

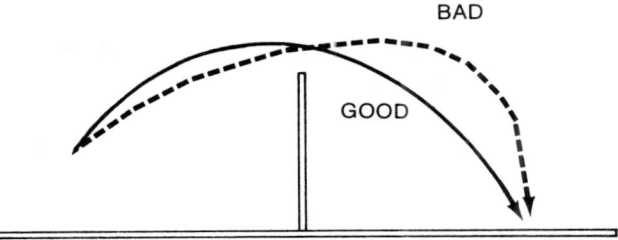

Proper and dangerous service trajectories.

over the net or so wild that it drives the bird out of bounds, you win the point.

How much you're able to do with a serve beyond just getting the bird into play will depend in large part on how well you're able to read your opponent and anticipate the response. If you see him or her obviously primed for a given reaction—such as running toward the net—or sense a momentary lapse in concentration, take advantage of it. If you discover your opponent has trouble returning a serving style or difficulty reaching a spot in the receiving box, exploit it.

Most receivers, you'll find, have much weaker backhands than forehands. If forced to hit a bird up on a return, they have only enough power to backhand it about to your midcourt, which is an excellent place for your resounding smash. An investigative serve to your opponent's backhand early on is always worthwhile in your service strategy. You may want to keep it up throughout the game.

There is no one magic serve. All can help you win; any can backfire and lose the service. The magic comes from consistency with the whole gamut of serves at your disposal.

Consistency is the most important quality you can develop as a server. If, through hard practice (aided by the drills you'll find in Chapter 5), you can learn to place the bird where you want it every time it leaves your service court, you've got a vital edge from the minute the game begins.

Ready to receive service: hand out for balance, racquet in upright position. *Courtesy Travelers Insurance Companies*

chapter 3
HITTING BACK

Once the bird is served into play, there are four basic strokes the receiver can use for hitting it back and which both sides can then employ as the rally heats up. These strokes are the clear, the drop, the smash, and the drive. They apply whether you are playing singles, doubles, or mixed doubles. Each can be hit forehand or backhand.

The stroke used will depend on the kind of shot you receive, your position on the court, and the position of your opponent(s). Unfortunately, you'll probably have only a split-second to decide. Because of the speed and deception that are such integral parts of the game, there usually is little chance in badminton for anticipation.

Still, in whatever time you do have, you should try to plan your return. It is not enough just to keep the bird in play; to the extent possible, you want to place it to your opponent's disadvantage. The better you select and execute your stroke, the more likely your opponent will miss the bird when it flies back over the net or unintentionally set it up for a kill on your next hit.

For the purposes of this chapter, we'll assume you are receiving a serve. Bear in mind, however, that much of the information we discuss here—the descriptions of how to deliver the basic return strokes, in particular—will be useful throughout the game, whether you are on the side that's serving or receiving.

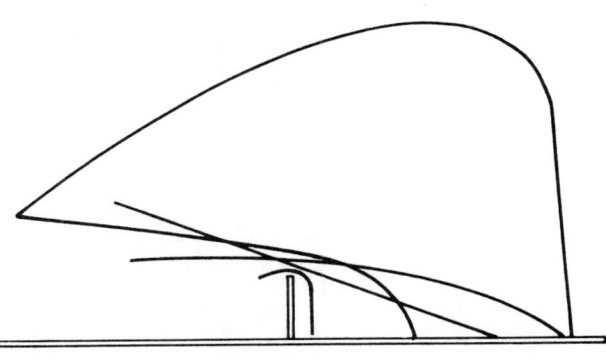

Ideal trajectories for various shots.

25

RULES FOR RECEIVING

To receive a serve, you must stand within the boundaries of the proper receiving box, with your feet being neither on nor over any line. You must hold your position until the bird leaves the server's racquet. Any preliminary feints or other efforts at distraction constitute a fault.

On the serve or any subsequent shot, you lose the rally if the bird hits any part of your body or clothing.

Only one hit per side is allowed for getting the bird back over the net. You may hit it with any part of your racquet not covered by your hand, and you may swing over the net *after* you hit the bird as part of your follow-through. But you cannot reach over the net to intercept the bird or touch your racquet, clothing, or body to the net in delivering a shot.

THE READY POSITION

In badminton, as in hiking through a mine field, you must always be prepared for the unexpected. As we explained in Chapter 2, your opponent in singles may without warning serve a typical low, net-skimming doubles serve, and in doubles you may suddenly confront the high, arcing singles serve. Consequently, your receiving stance should prepare you to run either back toward the base line or up toward the net to catch the bird before it touches ground.

The proper ready position is slightly forward from the center of your receiving court. Facing the net, extend your racquet arm at about a 70-degree angle so your racquet is in the air, ready to swing. You'll find it is faster to drop the racquet from this position to return a low bird than to raise it from a lowered position to hit a high bird. Your left arm (if you are right-handed) should be out to the side for balance. Stand with your left foot forward, knees slightly bent.

The ready position, followed by a deceptive drop return. (See also page 27.)

HITTING BACK

Keep your weight balanced on the balls of your feet, your body pitched somewhat forward, your center of gravity low. As long as you stay on the balls of your feet, you'll find you can dart forward to meet the bird or pivot quickly and sprint to the back of the court. If you try running backwards on your heels, you may throw yourself off balance and be unable to take position for a successful return. Be ready to move fast. Remember, the bird can come at you at more than 110 mph!

GRIP

Your grip will change as the game progresses, depending on whether you need to make forehand or backhand shots. While awaiting the serve, hold the racquet in the basic forehand grip. Your bottom two fingers should grasp the handle firmly, the top two slightly looser. Your thumb should lap over the handle, touching your second finger. This grip allows quicker finger movement than a vise-like clutch and facilitates the wrist snap most strokes require. To check that your racquet is aligned correctly in your grip, lay the racquet face along the calf of your leg with your arm held naturally at your side. The racquet face and your calf should meet in good contact.

WRIST ACTION

Tennis demands a firm wrist because the power of your opponent's ball can be transferred to your return if you hold your racquet stiffly. In badminton, however, if you try to bounce the bird off your racquet, you'll watch sadly as it merely falls to the floor. For badminton strokes, you want to impart power to the bird. The right wrist movement can help you.

The more supple your wrist, the more useful it will be. As you are preparing for a stroke, "cock" your wrist; that is bend

28 HITTING BACK

Below: Waiting for service, ready to pounce. *Upper right:* The forehand grip. *Lower right:* Taking a forehand with wrist cocked and ready to snap for additional power on the strike.

it—backward if you are preparing for a forehand or overhead shot, downward for a backhand or underhand shot. Then at the point in your stroke where the racquet is just about to hit the bird, suddenly straighten your wrist. The resulting snap adds noticeably to your shot's strength.

Sometimes, especially when playing close to the net, you want more finesse than power for a shot. Again, a supple wrist can help. In such instances, you want to move the racquet almost solely by using your wrist—a flick motion, with little or no arm involvement. With adequate flexibility and considerable practice, you can learn to coax and direct the bird over the net in seemingly impossible shots through this gentle wrist action.

BASIC STROKES

If, in speeding over the net toward your court, the bird is arriving on the same side of your body as your racquet arm, you'll use a forehand return, with the same grip as in the ready position. To handle shots aimed at the side opposite your racquet arm, use a backhand return. For the backhand grip, rotate the racquet handle a half-turn to the right (if you are right-handed) and lay your thumb along its wide side.

Within each of these broad categories, forehand and backhand, the initial movements for most of the basic strokes are virtually identical. This is an advantage you can utilize in making your return. You can keep your opponent frustrated until the very last moment, wondering just what kind of shot you'll hit back.

Where the basic strokes differ most is in their completion. Three require considerable power, one great delicacy—and all need steady practice.

The Clear

A clear is a high, arcing shot that travels in essentially the same parabolic curve as the singles serve. It can be played from anywhere in the court. With it, you send the bird toward the back of your opponent's court, where it drops suddenly on or slightly in front of the base line.

This return can be delivered underhand, but when possible an overhand stroke is usually more desirable. When hitting overhead, you are stepping into the bird, meeting it earlier and faster, with the advantage of forward momentum. And in badminton, getting an extra step forward on your return may allow you to hit back a winning shot rather than merely keeping the bird in play.

The clear is one of the game's power shots. Consequently, you must involve your whole body, including your leg and thigh muscles, in delivering it. If your body is coiled like a spring in the ready position, there's a release of stored energy you can transfer to the bird when you

The backhand grip.

30 HITTING BACK

Body and arm movements for the overhead clear.

Clearing from the backcourt. *Courtesy Travelers Insurance Companies*

straighten up to swing. Remember, your stroke must pack enough wallop to loft the bird high above your opponent's head almost to the base line before starting its descent. If you hit too short, the bird will land in your opponent's forecourt—the attack zone—and you may suddenly find yourself on the defensive against a powerful smash or elusive drop.

For the right strength and timing, move into the clear position as soon as you perceive the bird's trajectory. Let's assume that the path of the bird is high enough to allow an overhead stroke for hitting it back. Pivot quickly so the side of your body opposite your racquet hand is toward the oncoming bird—your left side if you are right-handed. Keep your feet shoulder-width apart. With the arm out, point your left hand at the approaching bird, simultaneously swinging your rac-

Sequence of photos illustrating the forehand clear.

quet back of your head with your right.

At the top of this swing, drop your wrist so the head of your racquet falls to the small of your back. Then with an uninterrupted motion, swing the racquet over your head, step "into the bird," and strike it just as it is about to fly over your racquet shoulder. Your arm and body should be fully extended. You should think of your stroke as throwing the head of the racquet through the bird. Yet *all* your body muscles should be behind your hit to diminish the burden on your arm and wrist.

As you follow through, step around so you can quickly resume the ready position. Your racquet arm should cross your body after the hit, with the top of the racquet head ending up at about your left ankle. You now need only raise your racquet to be ready for your opponent's return—if there is one.

In these seven photos, the player hits a forehand clear and returns to the midcourt position.

Ready for the clear from the backcourt.

34 HITTING BACK

Body movements and racquet positions for the overhead drop.

The Drop

A drop shot is usually best played from the backcourt. Done right, it just crosses the net, then drops sharply, leaving your surprised opponent scrambling to reach it.

Surprise is possible—indeed, a calculated ingredient of this play—because the initial position and movements, including the overhead arm swing, are the same as for the clear. It's at the moment of impact between racquet and bird that things change.

With the drop, you hold back. Instead of the forceful strike and follow-through used for the clear, you deliver only minimal power to the bird. Your body movements afterward should be just enough to get you back into the ready position, without the cross-body follow-through that brings your racquet head to the floor.

This delicate shot demands good wrist and finger control more than full-body strength. You want to do more than tap the bird, yet not wallop it. The trick is learning to match strength and distance so you hit the shot hard enough to get the bird just over the net—and no farther. And that takes experience.

The Smash

The smash, too, is deceptively identical to the clear in its early stages. But instead of the clear's parabolic curve, this stroke shoots the bird down like a bullet in a diagonal path toward your opponent's court. Smashes usually are made most effectively from the forecourt, although skilled players sometimes can deliver them from farther back, as well.

For a smash, you need a bird coming in rather high over the net. Move into the

HITTING BACK 35

The point at which racquet motion is stopped to impart minimal velocity to the bird—just enough to get it over the net.

36 HITTING BACK

Forehand smash: foot and body motions with racquet coming over the bird.

clear position, but adjust your timing so you can strike the bird a trifle sooner than for a clear or a drop. Keep your wrist cocked back and turn it slightly outward as you draw your racquet back. Then when you strike, straighten your wrist with a snap. This adds impact to the stroke.

Don't hit "through" the bird, like with the clear, but sharply and steeply *down* on it. Your arm should be fully extended at impact, and you should have the feeling of covering the bird with the racquet, with as much energy as possible behind the blow.

Follow through in the same path as taken by the bird, rather than across the body. This adds to the bird's propulsion.

When this shot explodes from your racquet with adequate power, it is one of the hardest to return in badminton for the average opponent.

Smashing a "setup" at the net.

38   HITTING BACK

A doubles player at the net, ready to smash. Although this man plays successfully without shoes, it is not advised for the average player.

The Drive

The drive is another power shot. It's flat and fast, just skimming the net. With a series of well-placed drives, you can send your opponent chasing from one side of the court to another. If you can keep it up long enough, he or she will tire and lag, then eventually miss one, giving you the rally. So that *you* aren't the one who tires, however, you must involve your whole body in delivering this shot. Drawing the force from your arm alone would prove extremely fatiguing.

Your position for the forehand drive is different from the other three basic shots. You should pivot from your ready position so that your back almost faces the net. Keep your racquet arm bent and well back, wrist cocked. When the bird is at net level, spin around rapidly and strike

The finish of a drive stroke.

it, using your leg muscles to help deliver the power. Your arm should be like a flexible instrument whipping through the bird. Follow through completely, so that you pivot back into position facing the net, racquet outstretched.

This shot is tricky, especially when hit from the backcourt, because the bird's trajectory tends to rise slightly as it reaches and crosses the net. If it rises too much, the shot can be more easily returned. Practice and game experience will help you determine when and at what angle to hit the bird.

Backhand

All four basic strokes can be successfully delivered backhand. Of course, the backhand is more awkward because it's harder to put your whole body into it. Therefore, you'll need more practice to develop the necessary control.

For the backhand smash, use the backhand grip and, if you are right-handed, pivot to the left while the bird is in flight so that *your back almost is turned to the net*. This accentuated sideways position allows maximum power and body involvement in your shot. Cock your wrist so that the fast snap in straightening it will boost your power. Your arm should be fully extended at impact, with the racquet head coming down on the bird at an angle that will deflect it sharply toward your opponent's court floor.

The backhand drop requires the same grip and back-to-net posture as the backhand smash. Reach as high as possible to intercept the bird, just as it is about to cross your racquet shoulder. Hold back on power and stop your stroke just after impact. As with the backhand smash, wrist flexibility is very important in delivering this stroke.

40 HITTING BACK

A shot vigorous enough to be a drop, clear, or smash. *Courtesy Travelers Insurance Companies*

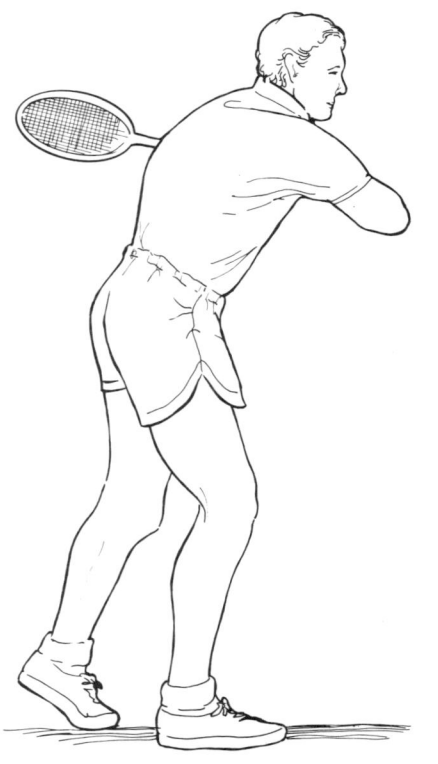

Step-by-step illustration of body and arm movements for the backhand drive.

Properly hit, the backhand drive can be a most effective shot, but it's hard to make. Again stand with your back to the net, knees bent, weight forward on the balls of your feet. Bend your arm bringing your racquet to about hip level and turn your wrist slightly so that the head is not vertical, but rather inclined toward your body. As you swing, pivot and snap your wrist, straightening the racquet just before you hit the bird. Try to connect when the bird is about a foot in front of your body. On follow-through, your arm should be fully extended in front of you, at about the "two o'clock" position. The closer you are to the net when taking the shot diminishes proportionately the amount of full-body involvement needed; rely more on your arm, wrist, and thumb to propel the bird. From any position, however, the pivot is essential for whip and power in the shot.

A backhand drive.
Courtesy Travelers Insurance Companies

Probably the toughest shot in badminton is the backhand clear. Unfortunately, you may have little choice in using it. A high shot to your backhand when you are far back in the receiving area or in the backcourt can only be returned with a clear or a drop. Facing that situation, avoid telegraphing your intention as long as possible to keep your opponent guessing.

The ready position for the backhand clear.

For the backhand clear, assume the standard backhand position. But as you bring your racquet around for the stroke, keep your elbow high, pointing at the approaching bird. When the bird is just above your racquet shoulder, bring your arm up and snap your wrist forward in making impact. In the backhand grip, your thumb controls the speed of the racquet, and you can use it to impart extra snap. Follow through along the bird's flight path, with your arm outstretched.

Arm and body movements for the backhand clear.

Timing, as in the forehand clear, is essential. If you strike the bird too soon, you'll cut down on the distance it will travel. Hitting it too late will drive it beyond the court boundaries.

Underhand

Executing underhand smashes or drives is impossible, but underhand clears and drops—both forehand and backhand—are useful shots in the badminton arsenal. They generally can't be delivered with as much power as overhead versions, but still should be a part of every game.

To hit an underhand clear when the bird is coming to your forehand side, turn your body at a right angle to the net, with your racquet arm toward your backcourt. Drop your racquet down and well back. Assuming you are right-handed, keep your left foot forward and with a slight rocking motion shift your weight to your right foot as you turn.

Underhand clear: advancing to the net after a drop shot.

Swinging up, strike the bird between your knee and ankle. As you deliver the stroke, shift your weight to your left foot. Follow through in the direction of the bird's flight, bringing the racquet back up to chest height. You can then bring your right foot forward and return quickly to the ready position.

To hit an underhand clear when the bird is coming toward your backhand side, pivot into the back-to-net position used for overhead backhand returns. This time, though, keep your racquet low and assume more of a crouch. As you swing, using the movement to pull your body erect, the sudden shift in position will transfer dynamic energy to the bird. Your follow-through will bring you back facing the net, on the balls of your feet, with your racquet fully extended in front of you. If you're like most players, you'll find the backhand underhand clear much easier than the backhand overhead clear.

Underhand drops, both forehand and backhand, are similar to underhand clears, except that the bird is hit when it is farther in front of your body. Keep the follow-through short and your grip a shade looser, to impart less power.

When you're new to badminton, you'll probably choose whatever stroke you think provides the best chance for getting the bird back over the net. Or, more likely, whatever stroke happens to pop into your mind when you realize the bird is hurtling toward you off your opponent's racquet.

But as you gain experience, you'll realize that, except in desperate situations, strategy must also be a key part of your selection process. When you're playing to win—and who isn't?—the ability to pick and deliver the right stroke at the right time, from your service return on, is vital.

Backhand movements and recovery position for the underhand clear.

Above: Backhand underhand drop. *Bottom left:* Forehand underhand drop. *Bottom right:* An underhand net shot in tournament play. *Courtesy Travelers Insurance Companies*

chapter 4
PLAYING TO WIN

While many of badminton's basic shots involve great power, rarely are games won on power alone, unless you are playing against thoroughly inept or inexperienced opponents. Power shots are tough to confront, but in many instances they *can* be returned by good players. An opponent who manages to intercept your hard smash and return it as a hard drive can slam your power right back in your face, perhaps quite literally.

What will bring you more wins than mere brute strength is finesse, that magic touch that makes badminton such a beautiful game to watch as well as play.

Whether in serving or receiving, you want to take control of each rally as quickly as possible so that your opponent becomes less an aggressive, offensive hitter and more a defensive retriever of your birds. This requires quick thinking on your part to choose the right stroke at the right moment and to execute the shot with the control and touch necessary to put the bird where you desire.

Deft, precise placement is like a ring through your opponent's nose. If you've got it, you can yank him or her all over the court, and then deliver an unreachable shot or force a return that sets up your winning shot.

Because there's so little time to think or plan during a rally, you should thoroughly understand the basic strategies of badminton before entering the court. The better you grasp the fundamentals, the more adept you'll become at reacting instinctively to the opportunities that arise.

STRATEGY

The strategy for winning at badminton can be reduced to a single, simple rule: keep the opposition moving, and when an unprotected hole opens up in the opposing court, put a shot there that can't be reached or properly returned.

The key, of course, is to manipulate your opponent(s) into making the kind of movement *you* want, so that choice areas of vulnerability open up. Try doing this by calculating your shots so your opponents are *forced* to run and swing in predictable patterns.

The specific strategy you use will depend on the strengths and weaknesses of the opposition and on the type of game you are playing.

Singles Offense

The shape of the singles court—five feet longer than it is wide—gives you a clue to the standard strategy in singles. Badminton players call it "up and back." That's how you try to run your opponent.

Whenever possible, alternate your shots. First send a high, arcing clear that forces your opponent back to the base line for the return, then deliver a drop to the forecourt. To reach that, he or she must run the full length of the court. If the return is successful, try another base line clear. Keep your opponent from returning any shots from midcourt, which is the attack zone.

Up and back is one of the most difficult tactics in badminton because the running and sudden pivoting are so physically demanding. Unless your opponent catches you off-guard with a return and then is able to break the pattern and turn the tables on you, one of three things is likely eventually to happen:

1) In returning one of your drops that falls close to the net, he or she will be forced to hit up to avoid driving the bird into the net. You can rush forward and smash this high return into another part of the court, where it is irretrievable.

2) In returning one of your base line clears, he or she will be forced to clear with a backhand. This is a very difficult shot for all but top-notch players. The clear will probably reach no farther than your midcourt, and you can smash it hard. The more shots you can get him to send to your midcourt, the better, because that's *your* attack zone.

Three examples of clearing shots. *Courtesy Travelers Insurance Companies*

3) He or she will wear out from all the chasing and simply be too slow to reach one of your drops or clears before it hits the floor.

You can make the pattern more effective by consciously varying it. If you hit several deep clears in a row, for example, your opponent may wait at the base line

expecting another; then deliver your drop, catching him or her cold. Similarly, a series of smashes near the net may condition your opponent for that shot; fire back with a clear to the backhand.

Another effective variance is side-to-side movement, as well as up and back. In chasing to the four corners of the court, he or she may become flustered or fatigued enough to return a short lob, which you can easily smash into some empty space.

Forehand recovery of a drop shot. *Courtesy Travelers Insurance Companies*

Singles Defense

Of course, any skilled opponent will try to manipulate your movements to open up empty space in your court that he or she can capitalize on. Your best defense against pattern play is always to try being in center court at the time the bird leaves your opponent's racquet, so that you are roughly equidistant from any spot.

This means that as soon as you return a shot, run to the middle. Make that your home base. Many players make the foolish mistake of standing still after hitting

Preparing for a backhand return. *Courtesy Travelers Insurance Companies*

to see if their opponent is going to miss their shot. This costs valuable time in the event of a return. You should try to reach center while your return is still in the air. Try *not* to be on the move while your opponent is about to hit the bird, because he or she will be able to see where you're headed and aim elsewhere.

Once you perceive the bird's trajectory, run fast. If you have even a fraction of a second leeway, you'll have a better chance of making a successful return.

If during a rally you begin feeling pressed for time and sense you're lagging dangerously behind the action, try hitting a clear or series of clears to your opponent's base line. A clear takes longer to return than any other badminton shot, and you can use it to find time for reconnoitering.

Doubles

Trapping your opposition into a pattern of play is much harder in doubles, simply because there are twice as many people to manipulate. Also, doubles is a much faster game and the shots are usually less

Speed is essential in reaching the bird.

predictable, which means even less time for planning and anticipation. Rather than a master game plan, you'll have to depend on, in many cases, keen concentration and hair-trigger alertness. Basically, you're waiting for the other side to make a mistake. When an opening shows, be ready to play it for all it's worth.

For example, if your opponents have no organized strategy for dividing up their court so that each has a certain territory, it is inevitable that sooner or later they will end up in roughly the same place to return one of your shots. Assuming you're alert to their position, you can hit the bird to a distant unprotected area.

Men's doubles: both sides using the side-by-side defense. *Courtesy Travelers Insurance Companies*

If one of them tends to play the net and the other the backcourt—a common practice in doubles—you can wear out the back player by chasing him or her from side to side with deep, corner clears. The doubles court is almost as wide as it is long; making a player run between the side lines can be almost as rewarding for you in terms of the toll it takes as the up and back movement in singles.

Try to avoid, whenever possible, hitting a shot directly toward one of your opponents. If you make a shot easy for an opposing player to return, he or she has more time and control in returning it. Even if the opposition must run only a little, you decrease the odds on a proper position for a strong return.

When you must aim toward a player, try for the backhand. The human wrist is constructed in such a way that a player's backhand is usually the weakest shot.

Always avoid giving an opponent a shot to hit down. When forced to hit up, he or she is on the defensive; when your opponent can hit down, *you're* in trouble. If you must return a shot by hitting up, make it high and deep to the backcourt, preventing a smash.

As soon as possible after a game begins, determine which of your two opponents is the weaker player and the exact nature of the weakness. Then direct as many shots at him or her as possible, tailoring them to that deficiency. Often you can score easy points this way. Or this may cause his partner, in desperation, to move over in hopes of intercepting a shot. Now you've got them both in one place and much of their court unguarded.

COVERING THE COURT

In doubles, the best offense often is a good defense. If you can keep your opponents from finding empty spaces in your court, the odds are overwhelming you can win the rally. Where your team's playing area is concerned, you should, like Nature, abhor a vacuum.

Clearing to intercept opponent's backhand.

This player is vulnerable because he has been forced to hit up.

To provide good coverage, you'll need a plan whereby you and your partner each have a "zone of operational responsibility" or "sphere of influence." In other words, you are each responsible for handling shots that come into your area, or sphere. This gives each of you some idea of the other's location and lessens the chance of collision or leaving some area unattended.

Dividing your territory should be done *before* the game begins. Each of you must know the system so you can cooperate properly. It's too late after the bird's in play to conceive and implement a strategy. Waiting will just result in chaos.

There are three basic approaches to covering the court. You should experiment with all as part of your familiarization with badminton and see which works best. Try to be adept at each, though, in case you are teamed with a partner who has a strong preference.

Front and Back

Front and back is an elementary coverage

system, often favored by novice players. One player covers the front of the court, usually from positions along the short service line or slightly in front of it. The other handles the entire backcourt. This arrangement is generally followed in mixed doubles, with the woman playing the net.

Its strength is placement of the net player in a position to intercept easily short shots and cross-court returns. Its primary weakness is that the players, especially the back man, can be chased from side to side by well-placed deliveries. If you play this system, remember to try getting back to the center of your patrol area between shots so you have a fighting chance to reach any return.

When possible, the net player should smash or drop high short shots straight ahead, and either drop low ones straight or direct them down the nearest side line. Returning a shot cross-court is generally a mistake, especially if your opponents are also using the front and back system, because this offers a neat kill setup for an alert opponent in the forecourt.

The back man should concentrate on clears, drops, or drives straight ahead or along the nearest side line, unless he or she can intercept a shot in the midcourt attack zone, in which case a smash is possible.

When this system is used in mixed doubles, the woman remains near the net even when her partner is serving, so that

Mixed doubles service: he's not holding the bird by the button, but it's still effective if they win the point.

she is in position to cover her territory the instant the serve is completed. She should stand almost in front of the man, near where the short service and center lines intersect but outside his service court. She must not block his view or that of the receiver.

In other doubles games, the player taking or making the serve generally advances after service to cover the net, while the partner covers the backcourt.

If you are the net player in front and back, never look back during a rally. You might get hit in the eye with the bird coming off your partner's racquet.

Side by Side

As the name implies, players using the side-by-side system divide their court along its center line. One covers the right side from net to base line, the other the left. Beginning and intermediate players alike can use this system profitably.

Obviously, less side-to-side movement is required here, but this strategy is vulnerable to up-and-back shots from the opposition. Again, your best defense is to try to move back to midcourt after each

For the mixed doubles service, the woman stands in front while her teammate (obscured by the television camera) serves. *Courtesy Travelers Insurance Companies*

shot. The one exception to this rule is when you have to run up to the net for a return. You should stay there until the bird is cleared by one side or the other, and then move back.

As in other doubles systems, partners playing side by side should be prepared to help each other during a rally. If you run to the net to return a drop, your partner should be ready to cover for you if your shot is returned with a clear to your base line corner. Quite simply, he or she must cover perhaps three-quarters of the court temporarily, until you can move back to protect your side adequately. Similarly, if your partner must retreat for a long shot, you should expand your coverage momentarily into his or her net area, as well as your own. Thus, while your moves basically will be up and back under this system, you must be prepared for anything, including sudden, demanding shifts from side to side.

Partners can help each other in other ways, too. If you see that a shot your partner is about to take will actually land out of bounds if allowed to fall, yell "No!" or "Out!" as a warning. If you're the one in back and you see your partner back-pedaling for a bird that you have a clear shot at, holler "Mine!" This prevents a collision and allows your partner to return to the unguarded portions of the court. Yelling at your opponents during a game is improper, but communication between partners not only is acceptable but often necessary.

Rotation

Rotation coverage is the most sophisticated and advanced of the three systems. It allows greater flexibility in play and usually permits the players to protect their court with greater success because the pattern of movement mandates proper positioning.

Think of your court as being divided into three triangles: a right triangle on each side and a cone-shaped or equilateral triangle with its base along the net. You and your partner each take one of the right triangles as your primary zone

Taking defensive positions in doubles.

of responsibility. In instances where a bird flies into the center area close to you or your partner, the closer one should take it.

Generally speaking, however, movement across the center and around the remainder of the court should be counter-clockwise; that is, if you are on the right and move into the center to take a bird, your partner should move around behind you. As play allows, each of you should continue moving in a counterclockwise pattern until you are on the left side of the court and your partner is on the right, and so on.

Moving in this manner consistently helps avoid collisions, but you should always know exactly where your partner is, nevertheless. For a bird that might be in contention, remember to yell "Mine!" to make clear your intention.

NET SHOTS

Whether you're playing doubles or singles, always keep in mind that while a badminton court covers either 748 or 880 square feet, you can quickly telescope the action down to within a fraction of that space. Indeed, championship players will often abruptly limit their movements to within a few inches of the net. Anyone who doubts that finesse and a soft touch are key elements of this game has never seen a superb player work the net with fancy shots. It's a talent that takes innumerable hours of practice to develop, but once mastered can win rallies—and games—time after time.

Many shots can be made effectively from close to the net—sharply angled smashes, abrupt high drops, side line drives, back corner clears. But the shots that are most impressive and often most telling are those in which the bird seems almost literally to climb over the net. To make these shots, you must combine the wrist flexibility of a Renaissance swordsman with the killer instincts of a bayoneter.

Here's how three of the fancy net shots are made.

Net Drop

The net drop shot is a maneuver that has little in common with the conventional, high drop described with the basic strokes in Chapter 3. Instead of the full power windup, the net drop demands a quick, faint, upward flick of the racquet—barely a tap—with enough wrist flexibility to lift the bird just over the net.

This shot is a good defensive response when receiving a high drop that is falling quite close to the net, but you are unable to reach in time for a smash or a high return shot. Facing the net with your weight forward on the balls of your feet, reach out your racquet with your wrist cocked to catch the bird after it has passed below the net tape. Use just enough wrist flip to get the bird up over the net. Ideally, it should reach the top of the net, teeter on the tape on its button, **and then fall sharply downward.**

Dropping a return shot from a kneeling position.
Courtesy Travelers Insurance Companies

Come as close to this ideal as possible. If you give the bird too much power and hook it too high over the net, your opponent may deliver a smash or a drive. But if it's low and hugs the net as it falls, he'll find a return difficult. This shot is particularly effective—and least risky—if your opponent has remained in the backcourt after having stroked off his or her last shot. Reaching the net in time for any kind of interception will be difficult; if a return is made, it may be only a high lift, which you can smash mercilessly.

Hairpin

The hairpin is a devilishly deceptive and tough-to-execute shot but, when done well, is a heartwarmer nearly every time because it leaves opponents in fits. You take the bird while standing near one end of the net and, with the proper wrist action, hit it so it travels almost parallel along the net to the opposite end, then glides over and falls near the side line. Your dumbfounded opponent is usually left standing close to your hitting location, wondering how the bird got so far in such a totally different direction than what was expected.

This shot takes a great deal of practice to develop your own personalized movements. Basically, you stand near one side line, your knees significantly bent, your weight forward on the balls of your feet. Your body should be at about a 45-degree angle to the net, with your racquet shoulder closer to it.

Try to take the bird on your racquet side between your hip and knee with an underhand motion, using the forehand grip. Your swing should be very short, almost a scooping motion, and your racquet head should be tilted back slightly to the right (if you are right-handed). Just before the racquet meets the bird, flick your wrist forward so that the racquet lifts the bird slightly and shoots it sharply off to your left along the net.

With practice, you can perfect the highly individual wrist movement necessary for the bird to travel parallel to and then cross the net near the opposite side line. In all probability, your opponent will have been watching your body or your racquet instead of the bird and have assumed you were using a net drop or slight lift for the return. Your success in outfoxing him or her will be a sweet moment, indeed.

Backhand Hairpin

When you are in a position to hit the bird in the opposite direction from that described above, you can use the backhand hairpin, an equally devious shot. In a sense, this is easier than the forehand hairpin because you can use your thumb in the backhand grip for guidance and propulsion.

Say, for example, you are right-handed and have reached the bird after it has dropped below the tape near the left end of the net. With essentially the same stance as in the forehand hairpin, bring your racquet up underhand in the backhand grip with the head tilted slightly to the left. Just before impact, flip your wrist so the head is more nearly vertical and make a short stroke to the right. Angled correctly and propelled at the proper speed, the bird will travel along the net and cross at the right-hand end, once again where your opponent is not expecting it.

As with the forehand hairpin, the movements involved require much practice to tailor to individual deftness, speed, and wrist flexibility.

ADVANCED RETURNS

To beginning players, some shots—the smash, for instance—seem like sure point winners. Often they are. Yet if you have enough time, these "kill" shots many times can be returned successfully and even used to gain the offensive.

If, for example, you perceive that your opponent is about to deliver a smash, you have a split-second to get into proper position for an interception. Try to face the bird squarely and drop your racquet from the ready position to about waist height, with your arm bent. Use the forehand or backhand grip, depending on the bird's probable trajectory. Actually, backhand is usually best, if you can manage it. age it.

There'll be no time for a full stroke, so when the smash comes at you, intercept it with a short, "punched" stroke, using mostly wrist flick and thumb push. With this blunt stroke, you may be able to convert the smash into a drive return or possibly a drop.

When facing a drive shot at your body, you may not have time to position yourself for a proper return. Take the shot as you can, even if you must bring the racquet around behind you or hold it head down between your legs! You may not execute a highly regarded shot, but you may be able to keep the bird in play and sufficiently disconcert your opponent to fault your return.

Anticipating a possible smash return of his partner's shot, the net man has lowered his racquet.

PLAYING TO WIN 61

Responding to a body shot with a short return.

The shots between your legs or behind your back are spectacular, but purely defensive. The important consideration is keeping the volley going. The behind-the-back shot is executed holding the racquet with the backhand grip, squarely facing your opponent with your racquet arm extended across your back. Use your wrist and thumb to propel the bird as it comes toward your left side. For the shot between your legs, use the forehand grip, spread your legs wide apart, drop your racquet between them from behind your body, take the shot—and pray!

These shots are sometimes necessary to handle a drive when you are off balance and cannot bring your arm back in time for a regular stroke. Remember, the pace of this game can be so furious that these may be the only responses you can make. If one of them works, it's the best of all possible shots!

TELEGRAPHING FALSE MESSAGES

Throughout this book we've talked about deception as the very heart of badminton. In particular, we've mentioned how body movements can fool your opponents—appearing to be winding up for a smash, for example, and then at the last minute reining your stroke and delivering a "fly swatter" punch to send the bird into a drop.

Skillful players often bring another deception into play—with their eyes. Many times an inexperienced player will unconsciously "telegraph" the bird's intended placement by looking at the target as he or she makes the stroke. This is quite natural, of course, since it helps to see where you're aiming! But at the same time, it inescapably tips off an observant opponent.

With practice, you can emulate experienced players by training yourself to look in one direction while actually delivering your shot in another. Developing peripheral vision can help you do this. But it is still more important to gain playing experience so you can sense distances and locations without actually sighting them head-on. With practice, this will allow you control on a shot without precisely looking ahead of it and trick your opponent into running headlong one way, following your deceptive eyes, while the bird goes another.

RELAXATION

A final tip on playing to win: stay relaxed. It's axiomatic in badminton that a tense player will be a loser. Remember, the basic purposes of this game are enjoyment and physical conditioning. Remember also, badminton is a lifetime sport, one you can play for many, many years. If you miss one opportunity to win, many others will come along.

If you are clearly outclassed in a game—and you'll know early out if you are—play your heart out anyway and relish in the exercise. Even in losing, you'll have learned something about your opponent and about your own game.

If you are closely matched and feel you have a chance to win, avoid focusing on your opponent's strengths. Search instead for his weaknesses and play to them. Concentrate hardest on the fundamentals of the game: stroke execution and strategy. This will keep your attention where it should be and help turn in a peak performance.

A return shot using a deceptive "fly swatter" drop shot.

Scooping the bird from the floor like a pro. The secret: position the racquet face at a right angle to the bird, then scoop it up.

chapter 5
DRILL AND FITNESS

Physical fitness is essential if you want to enjoy a game that's worth the time it takes to play it. A good contest puts a heavy load on your muscles, your limbs, your lungs, and your heart—in addition to your wits. While anyone is capable of batting a bird back and forth across the net, it takes a trim, lithe, well-conditioned athlete to get the most from the game of badminton.

If there's any doubt about your ability to withstand the strain of fast-paced games, you should check with your physician first. Beyond that, the degree of conditioning you'll need will depend largely on where badminton fits into your life.

RECREATIONAL CONDITIONING

If you're a typical recreational player, playing perhaps two or three times a week for several hours a session, you'll probably need no more off-court training than what millions of Americans engage in to keep themselves in shape. Each day you might jog a mile or so, do 10 to 20 sit-ups, and about 15 minutes of stretching exercises or yoga "asanas." All these conditioners will help your badminton game by heightening your muscle tone, limbering up your body, increasing your endurance, and improving your vascular capacity and circulatory reserves.

Avoid smoking, because you need maximum lung capacity. Eat moderately, because fat will slow you down. Don't drink before a game, or you'll dull your reactions. Get plenty of sleep, or you'll be too groggy to concentrate. It's all common sense, which most health- and fitness-conscious people are following anyway.

COMPETITIVE CONDITIONING

If your interest in badminton becomes more intense, the preparation needed before playing becomes more critical. Any age player can become a competitive player; tournament events are run for both sexes in all age brackets, including 60 and over. But the requirements for getting into condition to play competitively are more rigorous than for the recreational player.

In tournaments, you may get only short breaks between matches, instead of the lengthy opportunities for relaxation and conversation found in most recreational settings. On the court, you may face competition that will require your total physical exertion. You'll need more than just ordinary body conditioning for sudden energy demands and sustained strenuous play. Tournament rallies often last for minutes, with the bird crossing the net 30 times or more. Running up and back and side to side from one court boundary to another requires a lot. If you're not in shape, you'll find yourself losing to players of inferior ability, but greater stamina.

For competitive conditioning, convert the ordinary shape-up program into something more rigorous. Interrupt your jogging, for example, with occasional full-throttle bursts of speed. Select calisthenic and yoga exercises that require particularly tough stretching and bending. Most important, play badminton every day, or as close to that as possible—and enter every tournament you can.

Most knowledgeable players agree that one tournament experience, where you face better players and better techniques in an atmosphere of throat-cutting competitive play, is worth more to your growth as a player than 20 unofficial sessions.

MENTAL ATTITUDE

Many players develop the physical abilities they need to compete successfully, but they lack something psychological, which keeps them from becoming champions or contenders. They may freeze in play, be awed by superior opponents, or simply tense up so much that they mishandle challenging shots.

The mental attitude required for good performance is self-confidence—built, of course, on a foundation of practice and knowledge of strokes and basic strategy. There's much you can do to prepare for a game mentally, as well as physically.

If possible, observe your opponent in play before your encounter. Try discovering his or her favorite shots and any pattern of play. You can then work at avoiding shots your opponent likes and plays well and concentrate on the troublesome ones.

When you enter the court, try appearing calm and relaxed. Some players come across as very temperamental and may try to distract your concentration with histrionics. You may counter this by totally ignoring their dramatics, the opposite reaction they want or expect. Your attitude should be one of quiet competence and assurance, conveying the impression that this match is a job to be completed before you go on to a really important contest. Nothing is more worrisome to a very confident player than meeting someone across the net who is just as confident.

In doubles, try sharing a feeling of optimism with your partner. Congratulate him or her after a good shot, and offer quiet encouragement after a poor one. It's ill-mannered to maintain a constant stream of chatter on court, but occasional words of appreciation or reassurance boost morale and often draw greater effort from your partner.

PRACTICE EXERCISES

Morale and physical conditioning by themselves will win no games, of course. To win, you must couple these elements with a basic ability and a fine touch, which can be developed only by practice and drills. These terms are not synonymous. Practice refers to specific motions or strokes you can repeat by yourself or with a partner, while drills are formalized procedures and patterns of action, which generally involve a coach and a group of players.

Stroke fundamentals can be greatly improved by practicing with a partner, or by yourself on a court or against a wall. Practicing badminton shots against a wall may seem odd, but there is enough bounce to the button of most birds to allow it, and this is a valuable technique.

Draw a line on the wall 5 feet from the floor to simulate the net. When hit against the wall, the bird will come back at a variety of angles, permitting practice on forehand and backhand clears, smashes, overhead and underhand drops, drives, and serves. Try to pivot and stroke just as you would in a game. To improve your low serves, draw a second line on the wall at 6 feet and practice serving between the two. Wall hitting will improve your reflexes, proficiency at shifting quickly between forehand and backhand grips, ability to bring your racquet back quickly to the ready position, and wrist strength.

If you have a vacant court available, you can practice serves in a more realistic setting. Either recruit a partner to retrieve the birds or have an ample supply of them so you need not duck under the net to get the bird after each delivery. Work on developing consistency with each type of serve. To sharpen your aim, direct each delivery to a specific area of the court. Set up pie plates as targets, so you don't have to mark on the court with chalk or lift the varnish with tape. During each practice session, try each serve at least twenty-five times.

Delicacy of touch at the net is something else that can be improved with practice, especially with a partner's help. Facing each other, each one stands about 1½ to 2 feet back from the net near one of the posts. Gently stroke the bird in a low skim back and forth as you move to the other side of the court, then reverse your motion and work back, without hitting the net with your racquet or dropping the bird. This practice will limber your wrist and polish the fine touch needed for net drop and hairpin shots.

With a partner, you can also practice the alternating pattern of clears and drop used in the standard singles strategy. Indeed, practice for practically any stroke or playing pattern can be devised between you and another player. Either plan the session so that both of you practice or one acts as a coach. Be sure at the outset that the purpose of the session and the role each of you will play are outlined clearly.

DRILLS

In formalized drills, where there is a leader and more than one student, the leader specifies the drills and their sequence. The order suggested here progresses steadily toward more skilled play. Obviously, badminton can be played and enjoyed without formal instruction, but organizing or joining a group for drills teaches and reinforces the techniques of winning play.

Service Drill

Service drills can involve any even-numbered group up to six on the court at one time. Space will permit two pairs of players to serve diagonally practicing the doubles serve, and one pair to serve almost straight ahead practicing the singles serve, simultaneously. Emphasis should be first on proper arm and leg movement, then on proper delivery of the bird. For the doubles serve, stretch a string across the court one foot above the net and practice getting the bird between the string and the net tape.

Net Drill

The group is split and lined up on one side line, one half facing the other at the net. With an "opponent," each player moves across the court to the other side line, at a distance of about 1½ to 2 feet back from the net, skimming the bird back and forth with forehand net drops all along the way. After the line of players reaches the side line, the pairs reverse and return to the original side line, this time using backhand net drops only. Each player should have a supply of birds so if one falls the team can continue simply by putting another bird into action. This drill develops wrist control and eye-hand coordination.

Teacher Drill

The players line up single file at the back of the court, near the left side line. The instructor or leader, standing alone across the net, hits a high clear to the middle of the right-hand court. The first player in line runs to midcourt, hits the shot back with a forehand clear, and runs to the right side line. Others follow in turn. After all have hit, the instructor changes shots so all can practice a backhand clear return. This drill teaches you to run faster than the bird—a skill required in every game.

Four-Corner Drill

This drill chases one student at a time to the far reaches of a court by having him or her return shots hit to the four corners by an instructor standing across the net. The instructor first hits deep to the backhand, then deep to the forehand, next short to the forehand and, last, short to the backhand. The student returns all with the appropriate clears.

Team Drill

In this drill, there are six players on each court. Three are lined up about 1½ to 2 feet from the net, facing players similarly situated on the other side. Three more are lined up at the base line, facing base-line players in the opposite court.

For the first part of the drill, the base-line players simultaneously deliver drop shots to the players in the other court near the net. The net players lift the birds high back to the base-line players. In the next stage, the base-line players clear to the base-line players in the opposite court and the net players drop to each other. With so many birds in the air at once, it's a safety precaution to shout "Mine!" when you are about to take a shot.

Service Return Drill

This is a two-person drill for sharpening the ability to return a serve with a drive. One person serves the bird, the other practices hitting it hard and fast in a straight line directly ahead, using both backhand and forehand drive return techniques. The serve must be low enough to rule out a smash and high enough so that it need not be dropped or cleared to recross the net.

Drive Drill

The drive drill involves but one stroke. Two players advance toward each other from any place on the court, keeping a bird in play with drive shots to one another. This is good practice for keeping the bird on a level trajectory and maximizing wrist movement for speed and power.

Hairpin Drill

Two players stand on opposite sides of the net, cross-court from each other. Hitting the bird back and forth, each attempts to strike it close to the net and to direct it toward the opposite side line.

The bird's flight should parallel the net much of the way, crossing just before the side line. This drill is excellent for developing the extra wrist twist necessary for executing the fancy hairpin shot.

Practiced consistently and diligently, these drills will sharpen your playing skills and should make you adept enough for tournament competition. With the help of other players, you can devise other specialized practice and drill techniques. Indeed, the best ones will probably be those developed on your own to satisfy special needs that you identify from playing.

PREGAME WARM-UP

Because of the stress delivered to the muscles, tendons, and ligaments of your arms, legs, and back during badminton, it is always a good idea to loosen up a bit immediately before starting play. This will lessen the risk of sudden cramps, tendonitis, muscle strain, or torn muscles and tendons—injuries which occasionally occur during hard-fought games.

The warm-up need not be strenuous. Jogging around the gym a few times, followed by some sit-ups and knee bends is a good start. To further stretch your leg muscles, place both palms against a wall, then alternately bend one leg while keeping the other straight and pushing against the wall for a few seconds. This puts modest tension on and gradually loosens and toughens the Achilles tendon, one of your most vulnerable tissues.

You might also want to include the yoga Lotus position. For this, sit on the floor with your legs crossed, like an old-fashioned tailor. Carefully place one foot up on the opposite thigh and then, *very* carefully, repeat the procedure with the other foot. Once you can comfortably do this, try to join your hands in back of you, one arm crossing back over your shoulder, the other reaching up behind from your waist. When your fingers touch, bend forward and try to touch your forehead to the floor. This is an excellent exercise, but should be done with extremely modest intensity at the outset. Build up your use of it slowly, as with any other exercise program.

When you do take to the court, warm up further by volleying for several minutes before starting the game. This will loosen more muscles, plus give you a feel for the bird and racquet and allow you to practice some strokes before you need them.

chapter 6
CLUB AND TOURNAMENT BASICS

In keeping with its social origins, badminton remains today a sport that's long on conviviality and camaraderie. Savage as the court contests may be, its pervasive aura is one of sociable people getting together for a vigorous good time. This adds markedly to badminton's enjoyment, as does the fact that it is distinctively a sport of amateurs.

There are, of course, many people of "professional" quality, so far as skill is concerned. Watching them finesse birds, salvage "impossible" returns, and control placement with marksman precision is breathtaking and exhilarating. Yet they remain amateurs, in the sense that they do not exploit their athletic prowess for a livelihood.

Moreover, they are not segregated from others who enjoy the sport. In the typical badminton club, you'll find participants of all levels, from tyros to ranked players. This is one of badminton's greatest strengths. There is a constant interaction in play between advanced players and beginners, without the snobbery, personality cults, concern with chic, and crass commercialism that has overwhelmed some sports.

One can look at tennis for contrast: a sport that has changed in recent years from one essentially of pleasant, cordial relaxation to one in which participants seem obsessed with avarice and triumph. In many tournaments, the ritual display of tennis excellence, elegance, grace, and genteel conduct—a tradition of many years' standing—has all but been supplanted by an ill-mannered, circus-like atmosphere, featuring money machines who are boors on and off the court.

Fortunately, this fate has not befallen badminton. The best protection against something like this happening is to continue strengthening badminton's emphasis on amateur participation and control. That's where badminton clubs come into the picture.

FINDING A CLUB

As an organized sport, badminton in the United States consists of a network of local clubs, most of them affiliated with a regional badminton association. Each club provides its members a regular place to play (either free or at nominal cost), works to promote the sport at the grass-roots level and may, if it chooses, host one or more tournaments a year.

If you want to know where the club nearest you plays, you can get that information by writing the United States Badminton Association, Box 237, Swartz Creek, Michigan 48473, or one of the authors of this book, Irving L. Finston, Midwest Badminton Association, 1804 Keeney Street, Evanston, Illinois 60202. Either source can supply information about badminton clubs and the sport generally to schools, colleges, churches, community groups, and recreation departments, as well as to interested individuals.

ORGANIZING A CLUB

If there is no club in your area and you want to organize one, gather a small group of people who enjoy the sport and would like to play indoors on a regular basis. Then approach a YMCA or some appropriate municipal agency—a school with a sizeable gym, a park district, a city recreation center—and indicate your willingness to put together a badminton program that will be open to the public, without restriction or exclusivity. In a sense, you are offering to organize and run a public recreation program in exchange for playing facilities.

If you don't know the game well or would like help in getting your organization off the ground, write or call the U.S. Badminton Association or Irving Finston, secretary of the Midwest Badminton Association. These sources can refer you to an ongoing group or knowledgeable individual who will visit your club and help familiarize you with the procedures.

Finally, when your club is underway, affiliate with the regional and national badminton associations, so that your players can receive information about sanctioned tournaments. USBA members have special tournament participation and ranking rights and receive *Badminton U.S.A.*, a magazine devoted to news about the sport.

TOURNAMENT PLAY

Whether they are informal events for your own club members and other interested parties from the area or open, competitive contests which attract top players from many states, tournaments add a definite luster to badminton. There's a euphoria about challenging superior talent or meeting the challenge of others that lifts your spirits and spurs you on to play, despite mind- and limb-numbing weariness.

In the end, whether you have won or lost, you will have learned more about your own capabilities and the game itself. Even if you are no more than an observer, chances are that by seeing new players in action you'll pick up tricks which you can then inject into your own games to make them more rewarding.

Moreover, recognition within the sport comes from ranking, a formalized procedure based on individual performance in tournament play. Tournament results are supplied to regional and national associations and then are computerized to assign top players a designated evaluation, comparing them to others involved in the sport. Becoming skilled enough to earn a ranking is great for the ego, needless to say. But beyond that, the rankings are essential for seeding players in tournaments, that is, scheduling players in recognition of their ability so that they meet in later tournament rounds rather than in early matches.

Competitors seeking national ranking must belong to the USBA (membership about $20 a year) and should limit their tournament competition to events with USBA sanction. The USBA gives tournament endorsements primarily as a means of exercising logistical control, to avoid scheduling conflicts. The process for receiving USBA sanction can be obtained by writing the organization at its national headquarters in Swartz Creek, Michigan.

ORGANIZING A TOURNAMENT

Tournaments customarily are played over a weekend, but they generally require months of preparation. Almost all depend on voluntary help, and their success involves careful organization, planning, leadership, and control. At least ninety days lead time is recommended.

If you are designated to head a tournament planning group, you'll be responsible for supervising at least ten separate functions. What should be done, step by step, regarding each is too detailed to explain here, but a manual providing that information in easy-to-understand terms is available for $5 from the Midwest Badminton Association at the Evanston address listed on page 72.

This chart will provide some idea of what is involved. It shows the basic functions divided by committee, with a list of the general responsibilities of each.

TOURNAMENT STRUCTURE

Where participants and spectators are concerned, the most important part of any tournament is its structure—the formal system by which players and teams confront one another and advance or drop out of competition until at last only the winners are left.

There are four fundamental tournament structures: single elimination, double elimination, drop flight, and ABCD. We have described each to show how contestants should be matched and play should progress.

Remember, in a tournament there is usually a variety of distinct competitions—men's and women's singles; men's, women's, and mixed doubles; and, sometimes, junior and senior divisions of these categories. If court space allows, these can be run simultaneously. In any event, charts similar to those diagrammed will be necessary for each entrant category.

Single Elimination

This structure is quick and easy, the simplest type of tournament to run or enter. Lose one match and you're out. The principal disadvantage, therefore, is that contestants have fewer opportunities to play, unless they win consistently. Consolation contests can be run supplementary to the main action to occupy losers and heighten interest in the tournament.

Double Elimination

The double elimination structure provides more playing time for each contestant. You must be defeated at least twice before being dropped from competition. Also, even if you lose in an early round, you still have a shot at the championship because the losers' bracket parallels the winners', and the title match pits the winner in the winners' bracket with the winner of the losers' bracket.

Drop Flight

Drop flight offers more playing opportunity for each contestant than either the single or double elimination approach. Generally, you need at least sixteen entrants for a viable setup. It is quite appropriate, of course, to use this structure for categories with many entrants and a simpler one where there are fewer participants. It is not necessary that all events in a tournament be structured identically.

ABCD

This structure is the most complex and consequently offers the most chances for all contestants to play. The more action you can guarantee at a tournament, the more appealing it will be both for participants and observers. However, a more complex structure means more work for those behind the scenes.

For the player who really takes to the game, tournament competition often proves to be the ultimate badminton experience. Yet you need not feel pressed to participate at that level. Many skilled players never enter tournaments, preferring instead simply to play regularly within a club setting more for fun and exercise than for public achievement.

That is the beauty of this sport. Whatever you want from an athletic pastime, you can expect from badminton.

Tournament Organization

Committee	Function
General Planning	a) plan and coordinate all subordinate functions; b) establish entry fees and distribute forms; c) intercede at any crisis point.
Food	Purchase and serve light foods during tournament (soup, fruit, candy, sandwiches).
Communications	a) install p.a. equipment so control committee can communicate with all gym and rest areas; b) identify all courts by number; c) post signs for rest, food, locker, and toilet areas.
Seed, Draw, and Control	a) schedule matches; b) seed players; c) control flow of players and be sure all matches have been played and recorded.
Publicity	a) contact media, schools, and local clubs before event; b) get results of tournament published.
Trophy	a) order trophies; b) help distribute trophies to winners.
Finance	a) receive and disperse funds; b) maintain adequate records.
First Aid	a) provide emergency medical personnel and equipment; b) arrange stand-by medical transportation; c) locate nearest 24-hour medical facility.
Equipment	a) obtain nets, posts, birds, spare racquets; b) properly humidify birds; c) install netting and properly mark courts.
Transportation & Housing	a) locate lodging for visiting players; b) provide transportation to and from gym.
Banquet	a) canvass players for participation; b) arrange banquet at conclusion of tourney.

CLUB AND TOURNAMENT BASICS 75

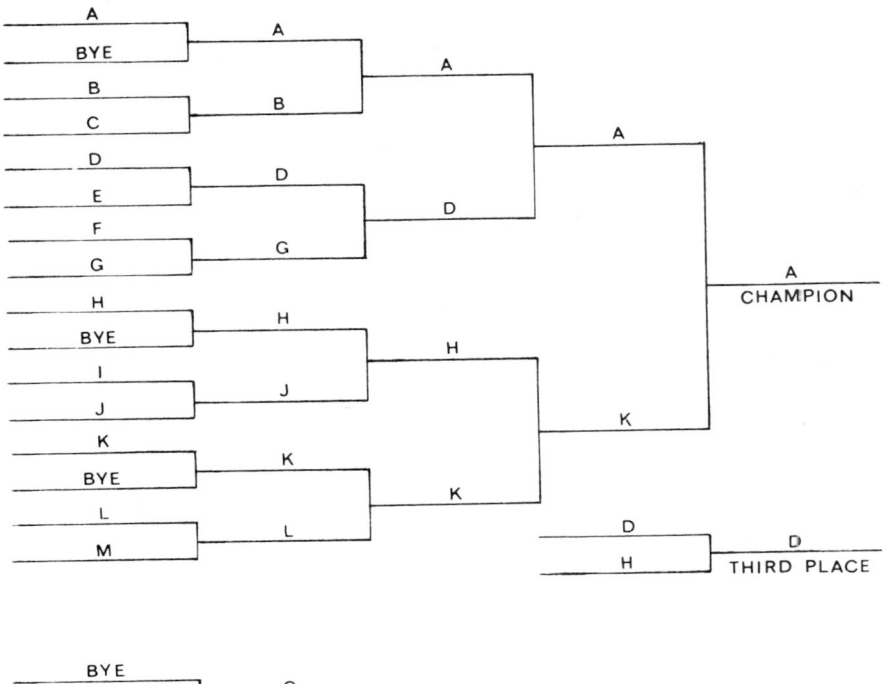

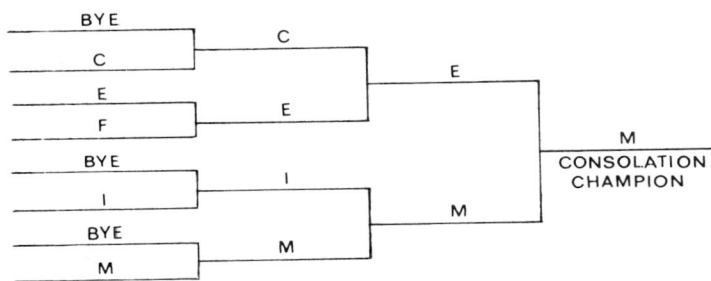

Schematic for single elimination and consolation tournaments.

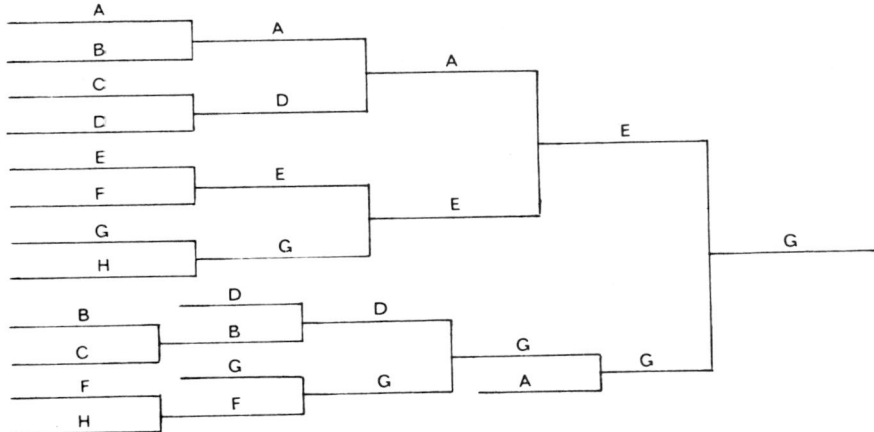

Schematic for double elimination tournament.

76 CLUB AND TOURNAMENT BASICS

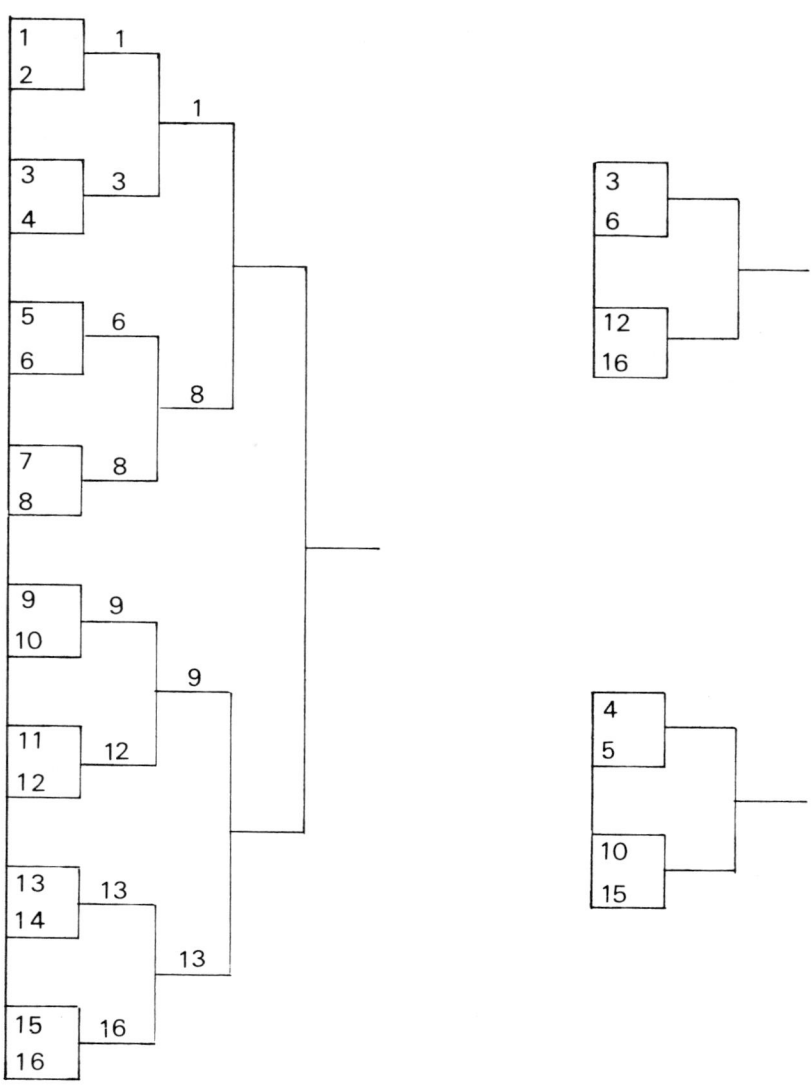
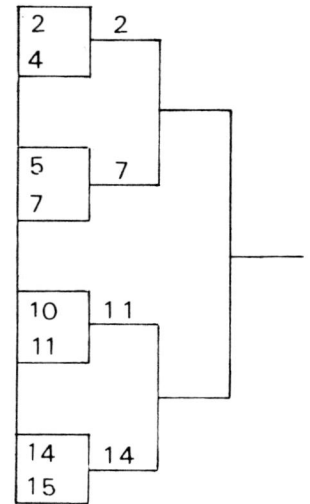

Schematic for drop-flight tournament.

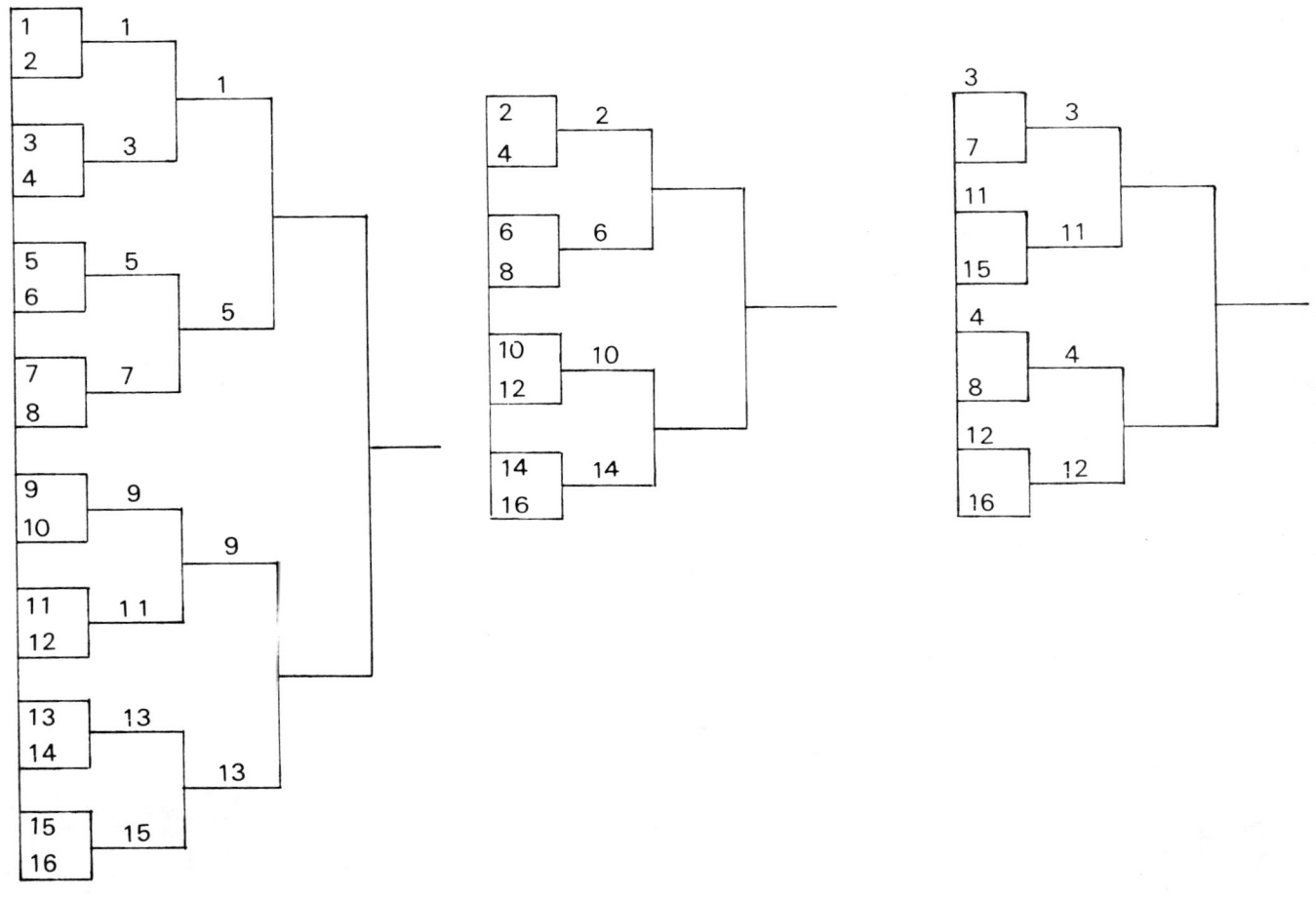

Schematic for ABCD tournament.

chapter 7
USBA RULES

Formal organizations to codify and supervise the rules of badminton and regulate its official contests have existed since 1893, when the Badminton Association of England was formed. Badminton became subject to international regulation in 1934, when the International Badminton Federation was founded by Canada, Denmark, England, France, Ireland, the Netherlands, New Zealand, Scotland, and Wales. Today, more than fifty national organizations are associated with the IBF, which, among other things, oversees competition for international contests in badminton, including the prestigious Thomas Cup for men and the Uber Cup for women.

In the U.S., the United States Badminton Association is the supreme arbiter of the sport, having recently absorbed and succeeded the American Badminton Association, which was organized in 1936. A nonprofit service organization, the USBA promulgates rules, sanctions tournaments, determines standards for amateurs and professionals, seeks to promote the sport nationally, and represents American badminton interests in international situations.

The following are the official USBA Laws of Badminton. For the most part, they mirror the rules of the IBF.

1. COURT

The court shall be defined by white or yellow lines, or, if this is not possible, by other easily distinguishable lines, 1½ inches wide.

In making the court, the width of the center lines shall be equally divided between the right and left service courts; the width of the short service line and the long service line shall fall within the 13-foot measurement given as the length of the doubles service court, and the width of all other boundary lines shall fall within the measurements given.

Where space does not permit the marking out of a court for doubles, a court may be marked out for singles only. This court shall measure 44 feet long by 17 feet wide, with the net across the width in the exact center. At 6½ feet back from the net on each side, a short service line shall be laid down across the entire width of the court. Perpendicular to each short service line and beginning in its exact center shall be a center line, reaching back 15½ feet to each back boundary line.

Space permitting, the court shall be marked for both singles and doubles play. This combination court shall measure 44 feet by 20 feet, with the net across the middle. At 1½ feet in from each side boundary line, a parallel singles side boundary line shall be laid down for the full length of the court. At 2½ feet in from each back boundary line, a parallel doubles long service line shall be laid down across the full width of the court. At 6½ feet back from the net on each side, a short service line shall be laid down for the full width of the court. A center line in the exact middle of the court shall extend from the short service line 15½ feet back to the back boundary line.

The height of a court for international competitive play shall be a minimum of 26 feet, or 8 meters, from the floor over the full court. This height shall be entirely free of girders and other osbtructions over the area of the court.

Where necessary on account of the structure of a building, the local badminton authority may, subject to the right of veto by the USBA, make by-laws dealing with cases in which a shuttle touches an obstruction.

There shall be at least 4 feet, or 1.25 meters, clear space surrounding all the outer lines of the court, this space being also a minimum requirement between any two courts marked out side by side.

2. POSTS

The net posts shall be 5 feet 1 inch in height from the surface of the court. They shall be sufficiently firm to keep the net strained as provided in Law 3 and shall be placed on the side boundary lines.

Where this is not practicable, some method must be employed for indicating the position of the side boundary line where it passes under the net, e.g., by the use of a thin post or strip of material, not less than 1½ inches in width, fixed to the side boundary line and rising vertically to the net cord.

Where this is in use on a court marked for doubles, it shall be placed on the side boundary line of the doubles court, irrespective of whether singles or doubles are being played.

3. NET

The net shall be made of fine natural cord or artificial fiber of a dark color and an even thickness not exceeding ⅝-inch to ¾-inch (1.5 to 2 cm) mesh. It shall be firmly stretched from post to post and shall be 2 feet 6 inches in depth.

The top of the net shall be 5 feet in height from the floor at the center, and 5 feet 1 inch at the posts, and shall be edged with a 3-inch white tape doubled and supported by a cord or cable run through the tape and strained over and flush with the top of the posts.

4. SHUTTLE

A shuttle shall weigh from 73 to 95 grains and shall have from 14 to 16 feathers fixed in a cork, 1 inch to 1⅛ inches in diameter. The feathers shall be from 2½ to 2¾ inches in length from the tip to the top of the cork base. They shall have from 2⅛ to 2½ inches spread at the top and shall be firmly fastened with thread or other suitable material.

Subject to there being no substantial variation in the general design, pace, weight, and flight of the shuttle, modifications in the above specifications may be made, subject to the approval of the USBA:

a) in places where atmospheric conditions due either to altitude or climate make the standard shuttle unsuitable, or
b) if special circumstances exist which make it otherwise expedient in the interests of the game.

U.S. rules permit adjusting the shuttle to obtain correct speed. A tournament referee or chairman is the final authority as to the need for adjustment.

A shuttle shall be deemed to be of correct pace if, when a player of average strength strikes it with a full underhand stroke from a spot immediately above one back boundary line in a line parallel to the side lines, and at an upward angle, it falls not less than 1 foot and not more than 2½ feet short of the other back boundary line.

Certain nonnatural feather shuttles are approved for use in all tournaments except:

a) Adult "Open" tournaments;
b) USBA National Championships (Closed or Open), and
c) USBA National Junior Championships.

5. PLAYERS

The word "Player" applies to all those taking part in a game.

The game shall be played, in the case of the doubles game, by two players a side and, in the case of the singles game, by one player a side.

The side for the time being having the right to serve shall be called the "In" side, and the opposing side shall be called the "Out" side.

6. THE TOSS

Before commencing play, the opposing sides shall toss, and the side winning the toss shall have the option of:

a) serving first;
b) not serving first, or
c) choosing ends.

The side losing the toss shall then have choice of any alternative remaining.

7. SCORING

The doubles and men's singles game consists of 15 or 21 points, as may be arranged. In a game of 15 points, when the score is 13-all, the side which first reached 13 has the option of "setting" the game to 5, and when the score is 14-all the side which first reached 14 has the option of "setting" the game to 3. After a game has been "set," the score is called "love-all" and the side which first scores 5 or 3 points, according as the game has been "set" at 13- or 14-all, wins the game. In either case, the claim to "set" the game must be made before the next service is delivered after the score has reached 13-all or 14-all. In a game of 21 points, the same method of scoring shall be adopted, substituting 19 and 20 for 13 and 14. (In all Championship play, 15 points is the official game, rather than 21.)

The women's singles game consists of 11 points. When the score is 9-all, the player who first reached 9 has the option of "setting" the game to 3, and when the score is 10-all, the player who first reached 10 has the option of "setting" the game to 2.

A side rejecting the option of "setting" at the first opportunity shall not thereby be debarred from "setting" if a second opportunity arises.

In handicap games, "setting" is not permitted.

8. MATCHES

The opposing sides shall contest the best of 3 games, unless otherwise agreed. The players shall change ends at the commencement of the second game and also of the third game (if any). In the third game, the players shall change ends when the leading score reaches:

a) 8 in a game of 15 points;
b) 6 in a game of 11 points;
c) 11 in a game of 21 points; or
d) in handicap events, when one of the sides has scored half the total number of points required to win the game (the next highest number being taken in the case of fractions).

When it has been agreed to play only one game, the players shall change ends as provided above for the third game.

If, inadvertently, the players omit to change ends as provided in this Law at the score indicated, the ends shall be changed immediately the mistake is discovered, and the existing score shall stand.

9. DOUBLES PLAY

It having been decided which side is to have the first service, the player in the right-hand service court of that side commences the game by serving to the player in the service court diagonally opposite. If the latter player returns the shuttle before it touches the ground, it is to be returned by one of the "In" side, and then returned by one of the "Out" side, and so on, till a fault is made or the shuttle ceases to be "In play."

If a fault is made by the "In" side, its right to continue serving is lost, as only one player on the side beginning a game is entitled to serve in the first inning, and the opponent in the right-hand service court then becomes the server. But if the service is not returned, or the fault is made by the "Out" side, the "In" side scores a point. The "In" side players then change from one service court to the other, the service now being from the left-hand service court to the player in the service court diagonally opposite. So long as the side remains "In," service is delivered alternately from each service court into the one diagonally opposite, the change being made by the "In" side when, and only when, a point is added to its score.

The first service of a side in each inning shall be made from the right-hand service court. A "Service" is delivered as soon as the shuttle is struck by the server's racquet. The shuttle is thereafter "In play" until it touches the ground, or until a fault or "Let" occurs. After the service is delivered, the server and the player served to may take up any position they choose on their side of the net, irrespective of any boundary lines.

The player served to may alone receive the service, but should the shuttle touch or be struck by his partner, the "In" side scores a point. No player may receive two consecutive services in the same game.

Only one player of the side beginning a game shall be entitled to serve in its first inning. In all subsequent innings, each partner shall have the right, and they shall serve consecutively. The side winning a game shall always serve first in the next game, but either of the winners may serve and either of the losers may receive the service.

If a player serves out of turn or from the wrong service court (owing to a mistake as to the service court from which service is at the time being in order) and his side wins the rally, it shall be a "Let," provided that such "Let" be claimed and allowed or ordered by the umpire before the next succeeding service is delivered.

If a player of the "Out" side standing in

the wrong service court is prepared to receive and does receive the service when it is delivered and his side wins the rally, it shall be a "Let," provided that such "Let" be claimed and allowed or ordered by the umpire, before the next succeeding service is delivered.

If in either of the above cases the side at fault loses the rally, the mistake shall stand and the players' positions shall not be corrected.

Should a player inadvertently change sides when he should not do so and the mistake not be discovered until after the next succeeding service has been delivered, the mistake shall stand and a "Let" cannot be claimed or allowed, and the players' positions shall not be corrected.

10. SINGLES PLAY

In singles, Law 9 holds good except that:

a) The players shall serve from and receive service in their respective right-hand service courts only when the server's score is 0 or an even number of points in the game, the service being delivered from and received in their respective left-hand service courts when the server's score is an odd number of points. Setting does not affect this sequence.

b) Both players shall change service courts after each point has been scored.

11. SERVICE

The server may not serve till his opponent is ready, but the opponent shall be deemed to be ready if a return of the service is attempted.

The server and the player served to must stand within the limits of their respective service courts (as bounded by the short and long service, the center and side lines), and some part of both feet of these players must remain in contact with the surface of the court in a stationary position until the service is delivered. A foot on or touching a line in the case of either the server or the receiver shall be held to be outside his service court. But if the foot is raised in such a manner that a part of it is over the line, but not touching it, it is not a fault. The respective partners, in doubles, may take up any position, provided they do not unsight or otherwise obstruct an opponent.

If the server, in attempting to serve, misses the shuttle, it is not a fault; but if the shuttle be touched by the racquet, a service is thereby delivered.

12. FAULTS

A fault made by a player on the side which is "In" puts the server "Out"; if made by a player whose side is "Out," it counts a point to the "In" side. It is a fault:

a) If, in serving, the shuttle at the instant of being struck be higher than the server's waist, or if, at the instant of the shuttle being struck, the shaft of the racquet be not pointing in a downward direction to such an extent that the whole of the head of the racquet is discernibly below the whole of the server's hand holding the racquet.

b) If, in serving, the shuttle falls into the wrong service court (i.e., into the one not diagonally opposite to the server) or falls short of the short service line or beyond the long service line or outside the side boundary lines of the service court into which service is in order.

c) If the server's feet are not in the service court from which service is at the time being in order, or if the feet of the player receiving the service are not in the service court

diagonally opposite until the service is delivered.
d) If before or during the delivery of the service any player makes preliminary feints or otherwise intentionally balks his opponent or if any player deliberately delays serving the shuttle or in getting ready to receive it, so as to obtain an unfair advantage. Any movement or conduct by the server that has the effect of breaking the continuity of service after the server and receiver have taken their positions to serve and to receive the service is a preliminary feint. It is a fault if the serve is not delivered in 5 seconds from the time that both server and receiver have taken their stance.
e) If, either in service or play, the shuttle falls outside the boundaries of the court, or passes through or under the net, or fails to pass the net, or touches the roof or side walls, or the person or dress of a player. (A shuttle falling on a line shall be deemed to have fallen in the court or service court of which such line is a boundary.)
f) If the shuttle "in play" be struck before it crosses to the striker's side of the net. (The striker may, however, follow the shuttle over the net with his racquet in the course of his stroke.)
g) If, when the shuttle is "in play," a player touches the net or its supports with racquet, person, or dress.
h) If the shuttle be held on the racquet (i.e., caught or slung) during the execution of a stroke; or if the shuttle be hit twice in succession by the same player with two strokes; or if the shuttle be hit by a player and his partner successively.
i) If in play a player strikes the shuttle (unless he thereby makes a good return) or is struck by it, whether he is standing within or outside the boundaries of the court.
j) If a player obstructs an opponent.

13. GENERAL
a) If, in the course of service or a rally, the shuttle touches and passes over the net, the stroke is not invalidated thereby. It is a good return if the shuttle, having passed outside either post, drops on or within the boundary lines of the opposite court. A "Let" may be given by the umpire, for any unforeseen or accidental hindrance.
b) If, in service or during a rally, a shuttle, after passing over the net, is caught in or on the net, it is a "Let."
c) If the receiver is faulted for moving before the service is delivered, or for not being within the correct service court, and at the same time the server is also faulted for a service infringement, it shall be a "Let."
d) When a "Let" occurs, the play since the last service shall not count, and the player who served shall serve again.
e) If, when in play, the shuttle strikes the net and remains suspended there, or strikes the net and falls toward the surface of the court on the striker's side of the net, or hits the surface outside the court and an opponent then touches the net or shuttle with his racquet or person, there is no penalty, as the shuttle is not then in play.
f) If a player has a chance of striking the shuttle in a downward direction when quite near the net, his opponent must not put up his racquet near the net on the chance of the shuttle rebounding from it. This is

obstruction within the meaning of the Laws. A player may, however, hold up his racquet to protect his face from being hit if he does not thereby balk his opponent.

g) If the shuttle disintegrates (cork and feathers separate) during a rally, where the cork strikes the floor shall determine the winner of the rally.

h) It shall be the duty of the umpire to call "Fault" or "Let" should either occur, without appeal being made by the players, and to give his decision on any appeal regarding a point in dispute, if made before the next service; and also to appoint linesmen and service judges at his discretion. The umpire's decision shall be final, but he shall uphold the decision of a linesman or service judge. This does not preclude the umpire from faulting the server or receiver. Where, however, a referee is appointed, an appeal shall lie to him from the decision of an umpire on questions of law only.

14. CONTINUOUS PLAY

Play shall be continuous from the first service until the match be concluded, except that:

a) in the International Badminton Championships and in the Ladies' International Badminton Championship there shall be allowed an interval not exceeding 5 minutes between the second and third games of a match (such interval being mandatory for all junior tournaments);

b) at the request of any player, a 5-minute rest period between the second and third games of a match, either singles or doubles or both, will be granted, and

c) when necessitated by circumstances not within the control of the players, the umpire may suspend play for such a period as he may consider necessary. If play be suspended, the existing score shall stand and play be resumed from that point. Under no circumstances shall play be suspended to enable a player to recover his strength or wind, or to receive instruction or advice.

Except in the case of an interval provided for above, no player shall be allowed to receive advice during a match or leave the court until the match be concluded without the umpire's consent. The umpire shall be the sole judge of any suspension of play and he shall have the right to disqualify an offender.

There shall be a maximum of 5 minutes allowed during a match for equipment repair.

There shall be only one injury time-out allowed per match (per person) and a maximum of 10 minutes allowed for such injuries. If a player is injured a second time and is unable to continue playing immediately, the match must be defaulted.

glossary

ABCD: A form of multiple-tiered tournament, accommodating a variety of skill levels.
Apron: Space surrounding the court, at least four feet in each direction.
Attack zone: The court area from which a smash can be safely delivered; roughly that section of the playing area from a point midway between the net and the base line, forward to the net.
Backcourt: That section of the playing area from a point midway between the net and the base line, back to the base line.
Backhand: A stroke hit on the left side of the body by a right-handed player and on the right side of the body by a left-handed player. The racquet crosses the body to make the stroke.
Backhand grip: The method of holding the racquet to execute a backhand stroke. The thumb is held along the flat side of the handle and is used to add strength to the stroke.
Base line: The back boundary of each court. Base lines are 44 feet apart, the full length of the court.
Bird: The missile hit back and forth in play; made of cork and feathers or of plastic or nylon. Also called shuttle or shuttlecock.
Button: The tip of the bird, made of cork or a rubberized synthetic material.
Center court: The area about halfway back from the net toward the base line, on or close to the center line.
Center line: The line extending on each side of the net from the short service line to the base line, bisecting the playing area.
Clear: A stroke which sends the bird in a high, arcing curve to the back of the opposite court and causes it to drop suddenly on or slightly in front of the base line.
Cross-court: A shot in which the bird crosses the net on a diagonal trajectory.
Delivery: The act of serving the bird.
Double elimination: A form of tournament in which each player must lose twice to be dropped from competition.

GLOSSARY

Doubles: Play in which a team of two players contests with a similar team.

Down: The termination of a server's right to continue serving, due to a fault. Each side gets one down in singles and two in doubles before the inning ends.

Drive (serve): A serve delivered with a flat, powerful trajectory from the side line of the service court, intended to land on the side line of the receiving box.

Drive (stroke): A very powerful stroke designed to propel the bird on a flat trajectory to the back of an opponent's court.

Drop: A stroke designed to make the bird cross over the net and then fall sharply on the opponent's side.

Drop flight: A form of multiple-tiered tournament.

Even player: The player in doubles who is always receiving or serving from the right-hand court when his team's score is 0 or an even number.

Fair-fall: A serve or return which falls within the court boundaries.

Fault: An action which causes a serve or a point to be lost.

Flick Serve: A serve delivered with quick wrist and arm motion that lofts the bird to the back of the receiving box.

Fly swatter punch: A short, quick stroke executed with a pronounced wrist snap.

Follow-through: The uninterrupted completion of the stroke motion after the bird is hit, which should bring the player back into a semiready position.

Forecourt: *See* Attack zone.

Forehand: A stroke hit on the right side by a right-handed player and on the left side by a left-handed player. The racquet does not cross the body.

Forehand grip: Method of holding the racquet to execute a forehand stroke. The handle of the racquet should be held as if the player is "shaking hands" with it, loosely with the top two fingers, firm with the bottom two.

Front and back: A form of doubles playing strategy in which one player is responsible for returning birds in the forecourt and the other is responsible for all shots in the rear court.

Game: The unit of play. A game is won by the first side to win 15 points in men's singles and in all doubles and 11 points in women's singles. By mutual agreement before play begins, a game can be set at a different score. 21-point games are common.

Game bird: A term used in play to indicate that on the serve about to be made, the game will be over if the serving side scores a point.

Good eye: The ability to observe a bird in flight and judge whether it will fall in or out of bounds.

Grip: A method of holding the racquet. Also, the portion of the racquet handle by which the racquet is held. *See also* Backhand grip and Forehand grip.

Gut: A natural substance, derived from sheep or cattle intestine, chemically processed into a filament and used in stringing the racquet.

Hairpin: A close-to-the-net shot in which the bird crosses the net at the opposite end from which it is hit.

Handicap: A concession of points made to a less-skilled team or player to make the game more nearly equal.

Head: The top of a badminton racquet.

IBF: International Badminton Federation.

Inner base line: *See* Long service line.

Inning: The duration of service before a fault is made.

"In" side: The team in doubles having the privilege of serving the bird. This team can score points or lose the serve.

Kill: A sharply executed stroke ending a rally.

Let: Allowance for replaying a rally because of interference or lack of preparation by a player.

Lift: *See* Clear.

Lob: A weak, ineffectual clear.
Long service line: The line in doubles beyond which the bird cannot fall on a serve without being a fault. In singles, the base line is also the long service line.
Love: Zero score.
Match: Series of three games. The match winner is the side that wins two.
MBA: Midwest Badminton Association.
Midcourt: The area about halfway between the base line and the net.
Mixed doubles: A game in which each side consists of one male and one female player.
Net: The obstacle over which the shuttle must pass in play. The net extends across the width of the court and measures 2½ feet in depth, the top being 5 feet from the floor at the center.
Net drop: A stroke executed from very close to the net in which the bird barely clears the tape and drops to the floor.
Odd player: The player who is receiving or serving in doubles when the score for his team is an odd number.
"Out" side: The team in doubles to which the bird is being served. This team cannot score points, but can win the serve.
Overhead: A stroke in which the bird is struck above head height.
Placement: The position to which a shot is directed. Good placement involves sending a shot to an area of the court from which it is difficult for an opponent to return it successfully.
Press: A frame with adjustable screws, in which wooden racquets are kept for storage to avoid warping.
Rally: An exchange of shots between players before a fault is made.
Ranking: A formalized listing of players by ability, predicated upon tournament results and published by regional associations and/or the USBA.
Ready position: The stance assumed while awaiting the action of play—racquet upraised, other arm to the side, feet apart with one foot forward, legs slightly bent.
Receiver: The player about to receive service.
Receiving box: The area within which the receiver must stand until a serve is executed and to which the serve must be directed. Also called receiving court.
Return: The act of hitting the bird back over the net in response to a serve or other of an opponent's strokes.
Rotation: A court-coverage strategy in which the players move in a counterclockwise motion as they return shots.
Rough: That side of the racquet strings showing the cut ends of the gut.
Rubber: *See* Match.
Sanction: A formal approval for a tournament, in the United States from the USBA.
Seeding: A process of identifying the most skilled players and positioning their matches to prevent their meeting in the early rounds of a tournament.
Serve: Initial stroke in a rally, putting the bird into play.
Service: The act of serving or the right to serve.
Service court: The area from which the bird must be served; bounded in doubles by the short service line, the center line, the long service line and the doubles side line; in singles, by the short service line, the center line, the base line and the singles side line. The service court is diagonally opposite the receiving box.
Set: To change the point total needed to win a game. Can be done to break ties or extend the length of a game.
Shaft: The part of the racquet connecting the handle to the head.
Short service line: The line 6½ feet back from the net, forming the front boundary of the service court.

Shuttlecock: *See* Bird.

Side arm: A stroke or serve executed with the arm motion more parallel than vertical to the floor.

Side by side: A form of play in which the players divide the responsibility for protecting their court into right and left halves.

Side line: A line indicating the outer dimensions of the court, perpendicular to the net. In singles, the side lines are 17 feet apart; in doubles, 20 feet.

Single elimination: A form of tournament in which one loss eliminates a player from further competition.

Singles: A game in which one player contests with one other player.

Smash: A stroke in which the bird is struck sharply and powerfully downward.

Smooth: The side of the racquet strings showing the smooth side of the knots.

Stroke: Movement involved in hitting the bird with the racquet.

Tape: The covering at the top portion of the net.

Telegraphing: The sending of unconscious signals of intent to an opponent through eye movement and body language.

Thomas Cup: An award in international badminton competition for men.

Throwing: Flinging or carrying the bird forward on the racquet strings instead of having it rebound instantly.

Trajectory: The angle of the bird's flight.

Uber Cup: An award in international badminton competition for women.

Umpire: An individual responsible for supervising the conduct of a match.

Underhand: A stroke taken from a point below the waist.

Up and back: A strategy whereby a player tries to run and exhaust an opponent by alternately hitting clears and drops.

USBA: United States Badminton Association, successor organization to the American Badminton Association.

Volley: A sustained exchange in which the bird is hit by several players before a fault is committed.

Zone of operational responsibility: An area of the court a given doubles player is responsible for defending, according to various established strategies.

appendix

American Badminton Association/U.S. Badminton Association Champions

Mixed Doubles

1937 Hamilton Law and Mrs. Del Barkhuff (Cunningham)
1938 Hamilton Law and Mrs. Del Barkhuff (Cunningham)
1939 Richard O. Yeager and Zoe G. Smith (Yeager)
1940 David G. Freeman and Sara Lee Williams (Skibbins)
1941 David G. Freeman and Sara Lee Williams (Skibbins)
1942 David G. Freeman and Sara Lee Williams (Skibbins)
1943-1946 No Competition
1947 Wynn Rogers and Mrs. Virginia Hill (Mosdale)
1948 Mr. and Mrs. Clinton P. Stephens
1949 Wynn Rogers and Mrs. Hulet C. Smith
1950 Wynn Rogers and Mrs. Hulet C. Smith
1951 Wynn Rogers and Mrs. Hulet C. Smith
1952 Wynn Rogers and Mrs. Helen Tibbetts
1953 Mr. and Mrs. Joe Alston
1954 Mr. and Mrs. Joe Alston
1955 Wynn Rogers and Dorothy Hann
1956 Finn Kobbero and Judy Devlin (Hashman)
1957 Finn Kobbero and Judy Devlin (Hashman)
1958 Finn Kobbero and Judy Devlin (Hashman)
1959 Bunky Roche and Judy Devlin (Hashman)
1960 Finn Kobbero and Margaret Varner (Bloss)
1961 Wynn Rogers and Mrs. G. C. K. Hashman
1962 Wynn Rogers and Mrs. G. C. K. Hashman
1963 Sangob Rattanusorn and Mrs. Margaret Barrand
1964 C. Ratanaseangsuang and Mrs. Margaret Barrand
1965 Robert McCoig and Mrs. Margaret Barrand
1966 Wayne McDonnell and Tyna Barinaga
1967 J. R. Sydie and Mrs. G. C. K. Hashman
1968 Larry Saben and Mrs. Carlene Starkey
1969 Erland Kops and Pernille Molgaard-Hansen
1970 CLOSED: Jim Poole and Tyna Barinaga
OPEN: Paul Whetnall and Margaret Boxall
1971 CLOSED: Don Paup and Helen Tibbetts
OPEN: Jim Poole and Mary Ann Breckell
1972 CLOSED: Tom Carmichael and Pam Stockton
OPEN: Flemming Delfs and Pernille Kaagaard
1973 Stur Johnsson and Eva Twedberg
1974 Mike Walker and Judianne Kelly
1975 Mike Walker and Judianne Kelly
1976 CLOSED: Mike Walker and Judianne Kelly
OPEN: David Eddy and Sue Whetnall, England
1977 Bruce Pontow and Pam Bristol
1978 Bruce Pontow and Pam Bristol

Men's Singles

1968 Channarong Ratanaseangsuang
1969 Rudy Hartono
1970 CLOSED: Stan Hales
OPEN: J. Honma
1971 CLOSED: Stan Hales
OPEN: Muljadi
1972 CLOSED: Chris Kinard
OPEN: Sture Johnsson
1973 Sture Johnsson
1974 Chris Kinard
1975 Mike Adams
1976 CLOSED: Chris Kinard
OPEN: Paul Whetnall, England
1977 Chris Kinard
1978 Mike Walker

Ladies' Singles

1964 Dorothy O'Neil
1965 Mrs. G. C. K. Hashman
1966 Mrs. G. C. K. Hashman
1967 Mrs. G. C. K. Hashman
1968 Tyna Barinaga
1969 Minarni
1970 CLOSED: Tyna Barinaga
OPEN: Etsuko Takenaka
1971 CLOSED: Diane Hales
OPEN: Noriko Takagi

1972 CLOSED: Pam Stockton
OPEN: Pernille Twedberg
1973 Eva Twedberg
1974 Cindy Baker
1975 Judianne Kelly
1976 CLOSED: Pam Bristol
OPEN: Gillian Gilks—England
1977 Pam Bristol
1978 Cheryl Carton

Ladies' Doubles

1970 CLOSED: Tyna Barinaga and Mrs. Caroline Hein
OPEN: E. Takenaka and M. Aizawa
1971 CLOSED: Mrs. Carlene Starkey and Mrs. Caroline Hein
OPEN: Hiroe Yuki and Noriko Takagi
1972 CLOSED: Pam Stockton and Mrs. Polly Stockton Bretzke
OPEN: Ann Berglund and Pernille Kaagaard
1973 Mrs. Pam Bristol and Mrs. Diane Hales
1974 Mrs. Pam Bristol and Mrs. Diane Hales
1975 Mrs. Diane Hales and Mrs. Carlene Starkey
1976 CLOSED: Mrs. Pam Bristol and Mrs. Rosine Lemon
OPEN: Mrs. Sue Whetnall and Mrs. Gillian Gilks, England
1977 Diana Osterhues and Janet Wilts
1978 Diana Osterhues and Janet Wilts

Men's Doubles

1970 CLOSED: Jim Poole and Don Paup
OPEN: I. Kojima and J. Honma
1971 CLOSED: Jim Poole and Don Paup
OPEN: Ng Boon Bee and P. Gunalan
1972 CLOSED: Jim Poole and Don Paup
OPEN: Eliott Stuart and Derek Talbot
1973 Jim Poole and Don Paup
1974 Jim Poole and Don Paup
1975 Jim Poole and Don Paup
1976 CLOSED: Don Paup and Bruce Pontow
OPEN: Roland Maywald and Willie Braun, Germany
1977 Jim Poole and Mike Walker
1978 John Britton and Charles Coakley

ABA NATIONAL CHAMPIONSHIPS

Senior Events

Men's Singles
1965 Dr. Charles Thomas
1966 Dr. Charles Thomas
1967 J. H. Butler
1968 Richard Mitchell
1969 John Leib
1970 Ted Moehlmann, Jr.
1971 Ted Moehlmann, Jr.
1972 Dr. Jim Poole
1973 Dr. Jim Poole
1974 Dr. Jim Poole
1975 Dr. Jim Poole
1976 Dr. Jim Poole
1977 Dr. Jim Poole
1978 Dr. Jim Poole

Mixed Doubles
1964 Larry Calvert and Jeanne Pons
1965 Robert Love and Virginia Anderson
1966 Dr. Waldo Lyon and Mrs. Helen Tibbetts
1967 Robert Traquair and Ethel Marshall
1968 Wynn Rogers and Mrs. Helen Tibbetts
1969 Wynn Rogers and Ethel Marshall
1970 Ted Moehlmann, Jr. and Ethel Marshall
1971 Ted Moehlmann, Jr. and Ethel Marshall
1972 Dr. Jim Poole and Mary Ann Breckell
1973 Dr. Jim Poole and Mary Ann Breckell
1974 Dr. Jim Poole and Mary Ann Breckell
1975 Dr. Jim Poole and Mrs. Helen Tibbetts
1976 Dr. Jim Poole and Mrs. Helen Tibbetts
1977 Rod Starkey and Carlene Starkey
1978 Rod Starkey and Carlene Starkey

Ladies Doubles
1958 Mrs. Al Kirby and Mrs. Thelma Welcome
1959 Mildred Sirwaitis and Mrs. Mary Connor
1960 Eleanor Coambs and Mrs. Hap Burdick
1961 Mrs. Al Kirby and Charlotte Decker
1962 Mrs. Al Kirby and Charlotte Decker
1963 Eleanor Coambs and Mrs. Hap Burdick
1964 Mrs. Al Kirby and Jeanne Pons
1965 Ethel Marshall and Beatrice Massman
1966 Mrs. Helen Tibbetts and Jeanne Pons
1967 Ethel Marshall and Beatrice Massman
1968 Ethel Marshall and Beatrice Massman
1969 Ethel Marshall and Beatrice Massman
1970 Ethel Marshall and Beatrice Massman
1971 Mrs. Lois Alston and Mrs. Beulah Armendariz

1972 Ethel Marshall and Beatrice Massman
1973 Ethel Marshall and Beatrice Massman
1974 Ethel Marshall and Beatrice Massman
1975 Ethel Marshall and Beatrice Massman
1976 Ethel Marshall and Beatrice Massman
1977 Rosine Lemon and Carlene Starkey
1978 Rosine Lemon and Carlene Starkey

Men's Doubles

1938 H. Henriques and George McCook
1939 C. R. Hutchinson and Leland Gustavson
1940 T. M. Royce and George McCook
1941 C. R. Hutchinson and Leland Gustavson
1942 Leland Gustavson and Frank N. Hinds
1943 through 1946   No Competition
1947 Lewis Rulison and Hulet C. Smith
1948 Frank N. Hinds and Fred Fullin
1949 Wayne Schell and Robert Wright
1950 Wayne Schell and Robert Wright
1951 Howard Holman and Fred Fullin
1952 Howard Holman and Fred Fullin
1953 Wayne Schell and Robert Wright
1954 Wayne Schell and Robert Wright
1955 Roy Lockwood and Dick Flemming
1956 Rupert Mee and Robert Traquair
1957 Carl Anderson and George Lane
1958 Wayne Schell and Robert Wright
1959 Robert Traquair and Ray Young
1960 Wayne Schell and Harold Seavey
1961 Wynn Rogers and Richard Mitchell
1962 Wynn Rogers and Dr. Waldo Lyon
1963 Bart Harvey and Charles Randolph
1964 Wynn Rogers and Dr. Waldo Lyon
1965 Wynn Rogers and Dr. Waldo Lyon
1966 B. Anderson and Robert Traquair
1967 Charles Randolph and Edward Spruill
1968 Wynn Rogers and Dr. Waldo Lyon
1969 Wynn Rogers and Lt. Col. Robert Gerzine
1970 Ted Moehlmann, Jr. and J. L. McQuie
1971 Ted Moehlmann, Jr. and J. L. McQuie
1972 Ted Moehlmann, Jr. and J. L. McQuie
1973 Dr. James Poole and William Goodman, III
1974 Dr. James Poole and William Goodman, III
1975 Bob Carpenter and William Goodman, III
1976 Dr. James Poole and Tom Heden
1977 Bill Berry and Rod Starkey
1978 Bill Goodman and Tom Heden

Master Events

Men's Singles

1972 Dick Mitchell
1973 Ed Phillips
1974 Ed Phillips
1975 Ed Phillips
1976 Ed Phillips
1977 Ed Phillips
1978 Waldo Foy

Men's Doubles

1972 Ed Phillips and Harold Seavey
1973 Ed Phillips and Harold Seavey
1974 Ed Phillips and Larry Calvert
1975 Ed Phillips and Larry Calvert
1976 Harold Thomas and Richard Witte
1977 Harold Thomas and Richard Witte
1978 Jim Wigglesworth and Jim McQuie

Mixed Doubles

1972 George Harmon and Bea Massman
1973 Bob Bachman and Paula Seavey
1974 Ed Phillips and Bea Massman
1975 Scott Garman and Ethel Marshall
1976 Scott Garman and Ethel Marshall
1977 Ed Phillips and Ruth Hoffman
1978 Ed Phillips and Ket Hoffman

Ladies' Doubles

1972 None
1973 Brenda Lumsden and Paula Seavey
1974 None
1975 None
1976 None
1977 None

Badminton Hall of Fame Award Recipients

1956—Joseph C. Alston, S. Pasadena, California
David G. Freeman, San Diego, California
Walter Kramer, Detroit, Michigan
Ethel Marshall, Buffalo, New York
Wynn Rogers, Arcadia, California
Mrs. Del Barkhuff (Now Mrs. Bertha Cunningham), Santa Barbara, California
Mrs. Thelma Welcome, Pasadena, California
1957—Hamilton B. Law, Seattle, Washington
Richard O. Yeager, Seattle, Washington
1958—Evelyn Boldrick Howard, San Diego, California
Zoe Smith Yeager, Seattle, Washington
1959—Helen Gibson, East Norwalk, Connecticut
1960—Janet Wright, San Francisco, California
1961—T. M. Royce, Seattle, Washington
1962—Donald Richardson, Waban, Massachusetts
1963—Mrs. G. C. K. Hashman, England
1964—No Award
1965—Margaret Varner (Now Mrs. Wm. G. Bloss), El Paso, Texas
Chester Goss, San Diego, California
1966—Mrs. Hulet P. Smith, Pebble Beach, California
1967—Marten Mendez, San Diego, California
1968—Mrs. Joseph C. Alston, S. Pasadena, California
1969—Beatrice Massman, Buffalo, New York
1970—James Poole, New Orleans, Louisiana
1971—Mrs. Helen Tibbetts, Los Angeles, California
1972—Carl Loveday, San Diego, California
1973—Donald Paup, Long Beach, California
1974—Dick Mitchell, San Diego, California
1975—None
1976—Sue Peard, Dublin, Ireland
1977—Wayne Schell, Massachusetts, and Robert Williams, New York
1978—Charles Newhall, Massachusetts

The Ken Davidson Memorial Award in Badminton

This award is presented by the American Badminton Association (now the U. S. Badminton Association) in honor of Ken Davidson, a world figure in badminton who was killed in an accident in 1954. The award, inaugurated in 1955, is presented to the player in this country who is judged to have made the greatest contribution to badminton and who has qualities of sportsmanship, attitude, and achievement similar to those shown by Ken Davidson. Awards are made in adult and junior categories.

Adult Award

1955 Janet Wright
San Francisco, Calif.
1956 Helen Gibson
E. Norwalk, Conn.
1957 Eddy Choong
Penang, Malaya
1958 Susan Devlin Peard
Owings, Mills, Md.
1959 Joseph Alston
Pasadena, Calif.
1960 Wayne Schell
Boston, Mass.
1961 Helen Tibbetts
Gardena, Calif.
1962 Ethel Marshall
Buffalo, N.Y.
1963 Lois Alston
Pasadena, Calif.
1964 Dick Mitchell
San Diego, Calif.
1965 Taylor Caffery
New Orleans, La.
1966 Mrs. G. C. K. Hashman
England
1967 Beatrice Massman
Buffalo, N.Y.
1968 Waldo K. Lyon
San Diego, Calif.

1969 Wynn Rogers
Arcadia, Calif.
1970 Ted Moehlmann, Jr.
St. Louis, Mo.
1971 Charles Thomas
Natchitoches, La.
1972 Stanton Hales
Claremont, Calif.
1973 Rosemary McQuire
Bristol, Conn.
1974 Virginia Lyon
San Deigo, Calif.
1975 Dorothy O'Neil
Norwich, Conn.
1976 Don Paup
Vienna, Va.
1977 Tom Carmichel
Ortonville, Mich.
1978 Chris Kinard
Calif.

Junior Award

1955 Robert Steinwald
Baltimore, Md.
1956 Marcia Dotson
St. Paul, Minn.
1957 Bernard Talley, Jr.
Baltimore, Md.
1958 Stanton Hales
Pasadena, Calif.
1959 Mari Beth Halloran
Minneapolis, Minn.
1960 James Lynch
Synder, N.Y.
1961 Barbara Bump
Greenwich, Conn.
1962 Susan Vening
Manhattan Beach, Calif.
1963 Lani Ferris
Baltimore, Md.
1965 Larry Saben
San Gabriel, Calif.
1966 Cindy Root
Philadelphia, Penn.
1967 Susan Wilson
Port Angeles, Wash.
1968 Nancy Bender
Wilmington, Del.
1969 Chris Burton
Port Angeles, Wash.
1970 Ken Nelson
Tacoma, Wash.
1971 Douglas Bender
Wilmington, Del.
1972 Sandy Muthig
Detroit, Mich.
1973 Cynthia Young
Pasadena, Calif.
1974 Bob Gilmore
Garden Grove, Calif.
1976 Carrie Morrison
Port Angeles, Wash.
1977 Kathy Ball
Ca.
1978 Lisa DeRouise
Wash.

index

A

Advanced returns, 59–62
Amateurs, 1
Attack zone, 55

B

Badminton Association of England, 79
Badminton U.S.A., 72
Button, 5, 8
Bird, 5–8, 21
    Aeroplane, 5
    Button, 5, 8
    Carlton, 5, 7
        Crown, 5
        "Fast," 7
        Feathered, 5–7
        Grip, *illus.* 21
        H. I., the, 5
        Humidification, 5
        Pioneer, 5
        Sportcraft, 5
        Synthetic, 5–7
        Yonex, 5
Backhand Serve, 22, *illus.* 23
Backhand strokes, 39–42, 52, 59, *illus.* 40, 41

C

Clear strokes, 25, 29–33, *illus.* 30
Clothing, 7
Clubs, 71, 72
Conditioning, 65–66
Court, 1–3, 10
    Boundaries, 1
    Doubles, 1
    Etiquette, 10
    Improvised, 3
    Lighting, 3
    Markings, 3
    Net, 1
    Outdoor, 3
    Singles, 1
    Service line, 3
Covering the court, 53–56
    Front and back, 54–55
    Rotation, 57–58
    Side by side, 56–57

D

Deception, 16, 62–63
Drive drill, 68
Drive serve, 21

INDEX

Drive stroke, 25, 38–39
Drop stroke, 25, 34, *illus.* 34

E

Etiquette, 10–11
Exercise, 65, 69

F

Fair-fall area, 14
Fault, 8, 23, 26
Flick serve, 21
Finston, Irving L., 72
Four-corner drill, 68

G

Game bird, 11
Game point, 11

H

Hairpin shot, 59
Hairpin drill, 68, 69

I

International Badminton Federation, 79

K

"Kill" shots, 60

L

Linesmen, 10

M

Mental attitude, 66
Midwest Badminton Association, 73

N

Net, 1
Net drill, 68
Net drop, 58–59
Net shots, 58–59
    Backhand hairpin, 59
    Hairpin, 59
    Net drop, 58–59

P

Power shots, 47
Practice, 1, 23, 26, 66–67

R

Racquet, 3–5, 8
  "Accepted," 3
  Carlton 3.7X, 5
  Grip, 5
  Metal, 3, 5
  Rules, 3
  Strings, 5
  Vicort, 5
  Wooden, 3, 5
  Yonex, 5
Rally, 8, 9, 51, 66
Rotation of Play, 8–9
  Singles, 8
  Doubles, 8
  Score, 8–9
Receiving, 8, 16
Receiving box, 21, 23
Receiving court, 13, 14
Returns, 25–45, 48
  Grip, 27
  Trajectory, *illus.* 25
  Ready position, 26
  Rules, 26
  Wrist action, 27
Rules, 8, 13, 26, 79–85

S

Scoring, 9–10
  Match, 10
  Rubber, 10
Service court, 13, 56
Service drills, 67, 68
Service line, 3
Service return drill, 68
Service trajectory, *illus.* 23
Serving, 8, 13–24
  Backhand, 22
  Boundaries, 14
  Doubles, 18–23
  Grip, 16, *illus.* 16
  Fair-fall area, 14
  First serve, 13
  Follow-through, 18
  Foot rules, 14

Legal racquet position, 14, *illus.* 15
Return, 14–16
Rules, 13
Singles, 14–18
Stance, 16
Standard, 20
Strategy, 23
Strokes, 13
Swing, 16
Shuttlecock, *see Bird*
Shoes, 7
Smash return, 21, 34–38, *illus.* 36
Strategy, 43, 47–58
    Doubles, 51–53
    Side to side, 50
    Singles defense, 50, 51
    Singles offense, 48–50
    Up and back, 48
Strings, Ashaway nylon, 5
Stroke fundamentals, 66–67

T

Teacher drill, 68
Team drill, 68
Tennis *vs.* Badminton, 7–8

Thomas Cup, 79
Tournament, 71–77
    ABCD, 74, *illus.* 77
    Conditioning, 66
    Double elimination, 73, *illus.* 75
    Drop flight, 73–74, *illus.* 76
    Etiquette, 11
    Lead time, 73
    Organizing, 73
    Play, 73
    Single elimination, 73, *illus.* 75

U

Uber cup, 79
U.S. Badminton Association, 5, 72–73, 79–85
U.S.B.A. Laws of Badminton, *see Rules*
Umpire, 11
Underhand strokes, 42–43

V-W-Y

Volley, 62
Warmup, pre-game, 69
YMCA, 72